D0209148

THE
RED ZONE

Cars, Cows, and Coaches
The Life and Good Times of a
Texas Dealmaker

Red McCombs
WITH MICKEY HERSKOWITZ

EAKIN PRESS ❧ Austin, Texas

FIRST EDITION
Copyright © 2002
By Red McCombs
Published in the United States of America
By Eakin Press
A Division of Sunbelt Media, Inc.
P.O. Drawer 90159 ▭ Austin, Texas 78709-0159
email: sales@eakinpress.com
▭ website: www.eakinpress.com ▭
ALL RIGHTS RESERVED.
1 2 3 4 5 6 7 8 9
1-57168-707-6

Library of Congress Cataloging-in-Publication Data

McCombs, Red
   The Red Zone. : cars, cows and coaches : my life and good times /
Red McCombs with Mickey Herskowitz.– 1st ed.
      p.   cm.
   Includes index.
   ISBN 1-57168-707-6 (HB : alk. paper)
   1. McCombs, Red, 1927- . 2. Buisnessmen–Texas–Biography. I.
Herskowitz, Mickey. II. Title.
HC102.5.M33 A3 2002
338'.04'092–dc21   2002008445

To Charline and the Girls and the "Blood"—
they know who they are and what they mean to me.

CONTENTS

FOREWORD

BY JAMES MICHENER

(Editor's note: This essay was one of the last dictated by Mr. Michener before his death in Austin, where he had been a writer in residence at the University of Texas.)

When I arrived in Texas in 1981 to research my historical novel of the same name, I did so at the insistence of the then Republican governor, William Clements, a persuasive fellow. The research alone went on for more than thirty months, and Clements provided everything I asked for and more: Access to the University of Texas faculty and history departments, at least a dozen research assistants and interns, a convenient place to live and an office where I could work.

After I had flown down for a get-acquainted visit, the governor held a dinner in my honor at the mansion, and all of the prominent lady Republicans were there to offer the loan of their airplanes, their libraries and office space.

At the end of the evening, which impressed me greatly, I was approached by a stocky man in his early forties, whose name I never did learn. He took me aside and said, "Mr. Michener, you are off to a wonderful start. You had all the leading Republicans vowing to help you out. But you must remember that three years ago, these same people were the leading Democrats."

This was my introduction to the shifting sands of Texas politics and culture. The state was then at the crest of the oil and real estate boom, and everyone seemed to be rolling in money. By the time I had finished my novel, the boom was over and the crash had wiped out countless oil companies and land developers and ranchers. There were six or seven massive office buildings in Austin and Houston, newly finished, with no tenants. They were referred to as "see-throughs."

But the downturn had not yet been predicted, and we were slow to appreciate the depth of the disaster, so the times were still upbeat and unspoiled. As I settled into my project, I asked around for the names of some of the state's major players. One of the names that kept coming back to me was Red McCombs. Not B. J. and certainly not Billy Joe, but simply Red or, as several preferred, Big Red.

By then he had been established as the first or second leading Ford dealer in the country, and had owned the San Antonio Spurs and Denver Nuggets of the National Basketball Association, and would own the Spurs a second time. He was in cars, cattle, oil and sports, and this combination pleased me because the people in sports, no matter how they isolate themselves and defy change, reflect the outside world. They reflect it in a way that makes writing about them relatively easy, because they conduct a large portion of their business in plain view.

And, with certain exceptions, they have a high boiling point when it comes to taking offense at what you say.

McCombs was easy to know, as I had been assured,

and he struck me as being close to the stereotypical Texan – a large man, still reddish haired, with a voice that would rattle windows. He was open and colorful and answered questions in exquisite detail.

Aside from his diverse interests and holdings, I was interested in McCombs because he had, almost single-handedly, created a market in the mid-1970s for the Texas longhorns, a breed that almost died out in the early 1900s. The cattle embodied the Lone Star mystique, but had a reputation for toughness, both in temperament and in its meat.

"Texas longhorns are what we call 'easy keepers,'" Red told me. "They are essentially disease resistant. They live longer. They calve longer. They're productive longer."

Other than providing endless generations of Bevos (the mascot of the University of Texas football team), the main value of the longhorns seemed to be nostalgia. They were relics of the Old West, and with their splendid and sometimes magnificent horns fun to "look at," admired by weekend guests to the ranch.

They had an exotic history, first brought to the missions by the Spaniards in the 1500s. It wasn't until after the Civil War that anyone paid attention to them, when the trail rides to Dodge and Chisholm came into vogue.

Red was riding high. He had founded the Texas Legacy Show and Sale in 1983 with Charlie Schreiner III, known as Charlie Three, owner of the YO Ranch. This black tie and boots auction and gala helped restore the popularity of the longhorns with breeders. Red was selling for an average of around $5,000 stock that a year or so earlier had gone in the hundreds.

He syndicated his prized, four-year-old red and white bull, Redmac Beau Butler, for a record price of $1.5 million. I watched him market his cattle as no one had done before, and I was there for the flowering and the fall. He handled each posture with style, riding the wave right to the top and all the way down.

In the end, what scuttled the operation was the Reform Act of 1986, which took the depreciation schedules out of breeding stock. Then the bottom fell out for car dealers, beer barons, and land developers. All the extra money was gone. But Red had the right theory. The longhorns had been in short supply, and he created a demand.

McCombs, and his partners, made the claim that longhorn beef was low in cholesterol, and then the research people at Texas A&M went to work and made the claim come true.

All during this time, my wife Morrie and I were entertained at dinner on half a dozen occasions by Red and his lovely Charline, at their 5,000-acre ranch near Johnson City. Once, they invited six couples to join us for a dinner on the patio and, on short notice, Red decided to hire the Johnson City band, made up of local musicians.

As it happened, the band was on vacation, but he persisted, as he often did. He called the band director and asked if he could get a small ensemble together. "This is Red McCombs," he began, and the conductor stopped him with, "Yeah, and I'm John F. Kennedy."

"Well, this really is Red McCombs and I'm one of your taxpayers. I just wanted to see if you can do me a favor." When he heard the request, the gentleman said, "You mean James Michener, the author? He's coming to your ranch?"

Red assured him this was so and added, "All we need is a small ensemble to play a little dinner music for fifteen minutes or so."

"What kind of music does he like?"

"Hell, I don't know. Whatever you can play. Whatever you can put together. Doesn't matter."

The guests were all gathered around the pool, sipping their margaritas, when suddenly you heard the sound of music coming from the driveway. Here came sixty or seventy high school and college kids playing "The Yellow Rose of Texas." My wife and I liked it so much, I asked them to play it again.

It was a lovely evening and revealed to me more of the character of the natives of this remarkable state. I was fascinated by what I found to be stereotypical in Texans. The difference really between Texas and, say, Montana, is that Texas was once a free nation and joined the United States on its own terms. Texas had five vicious battles against Santa Anna and lost four of them. The Texans won at San Jacinto, and in the end that was the only battle that counted.

But what really separates them is the fact that Texans believe they are different. I do not know what Montana's principal claim to fame is, but I doubt you will hear anything on radio in Montana boasting about Custer's defeat at Little Big Horn.

In the matter of cattle ranching, my mentor was McCombs at a very high level. He arranged for me to meet six billionaires. I interviewed them all, and by the time my book was published, five had taken Chapter 11.

ACKNOWLEDGMENTS

Once you make the decision to put your life—or most of it—in print, you welcome all the help you can get. By the end of the process, it would take a separate book to thank all the people who helped you to create a book.

The list is long of friends who contributed their opinions and recollections—Gary Woods, Lowry Mays, Henry Cisneros, Dr. Mickey LeMaistre, to name four. Many played a role in the events described in these pages.

The indispensable person in this project was Suzy Thomas, my always unflappable assistant for the past twenty-eight years, who controlled the traffic, worked the phones, and guarded the research.

A very special and poignant appreciation is owed to the late Ed Eakin, whose death in February of 2002, from a heart attack, was a loss not only to the world of publishing but to the enduring ideal of family-owned businesses. Ed pursued this book for several years in his quiet, persistent and courtly way, and ours was one of the last contracts he drafted for Eakin Press. Ed was dedicated to Texas writers and Texas history.

I am grateful for the efforts of his daughter, Virginia Messer, in moving the book through the final stages, in a difficult time, and to Melissa Locke Roberts, for her diligent copyediting.

CHAPTER 1

SPUR, TEXAS

I was born in 1927, the year Charles Lindbergh flew alone across the Atlantic, Babe Ruth hit sixty home runs, Ford discontinued the Model T, the Great Depression had America by the throat, and the song that may have best reflected the times was "Brother Can You Spare a Dime?"

My earliest memories are of the house we rented and then bought in Spur, a small farming and ranching town in West Texas. The white frame house had three bedrooms and one bath. I would have been seven when my dad, Willie Nathan McCombs, known as Slim, signed the papers in 1934. It was a pretty little house by the standards of that day. The purchase price was $900, the payments were $25 a month, and I remember my parents gravely discussing whether they could meet the notes.

The seller was Clifford B. Jones, who had property in town and had gone on to become president of Texas Tech College.

At one time, Spur was an interesting speck on the map, a quiet, well-behaved town of maybe 2,000 citizens, most of them churchgoers. Eighty percent of my schoolmates lived on farms and ranches, and a good many of them rode horses to school and tied them to a hitching post. We didn't know what discrimination was.

In that vast area, Spur was a hub for supplying the big ranches, and a train ran through it. Well, not all the way through it. The train actually made a U-turn and headed east, hauling its cargo of cattle from the ranches.

My dad was born in Groveton, near Lufkin in East Texas, in the rural area known as the Piney Woods. He was the eldest of nine children, and his family had migrated from Mississippi. All he ever attended was a one-room country school, which he left in the third grade to help work the forty acres they sharecropped and to earn extra cash by cutting timber.

The word had spread that if you headed west, families could sharecrop as many acres as they wanted, as much as 300 acres. But it was hard scrabble land, subject to frequent drought.

I once asked my father why he left the lush greenery of East Texas to settle in a place where it never rained. He said, "Well, we didn't know that until we got there." They rode in a railroad boxcar and got off at Spur, the end of the line. With his father, brothers, and sisters, he worked that dry, rocky farmland until he was nineteen, when he talked the local Ford dealer into letting him become an apprentice mechanic. He worked two years for room and board and tobacco, before he drew a paycheck.

My mother, Gladys McCombs, was from a family of farmers in Central Texas, who had known far better economic circumstances than the McCombs clan. Mom was a high school graduate and a bit of a snob about it. Her father settled in a pretty fertile area near Jayton, about twenty miles from Spur. She and Dad met at a country dance and married when he was twenty-five and she was twenty.

My dad taught me that the greatest gift a father can give his children is to love their mother. He also set high standards for loyalty, and I may have fallen short of his expectations in this regard, at least when it came to my association with the Ford Motor Company. (He disapproved when I bailed out of the Edsel, three months after that ill-fated car hit the marketplace in 1957. He chided me, but gently, the only way he did anything, over my short-sightedness. He reminded me that they had "a lot of smart people at Ford" who surely knew what they were doing, and I only needed to give the model more time. I thought three months of trying to sell the Edsel was darned near a life sentence.)

Over the years, I have been described as a long, tall, typical Texan, a wheeler (and car) dealer, who dabbled in cattle, oil and gas, broadcasting, race horses, motion pictures, real estate, politics, minor league baseball, and pro basketball—owning a majority interest in the San Antonio Spurs twice and the Denver Nuggets once.

I am not sure I qualify as a typical anything. But I love Texas, as a place and as a state of mind, and I can't imagine living anywhere else or doing anything but the things I have done.

Of course, the tales of former children are not always to be trusted. Some people supply themselves with too many victories, while others cling to hard times, real or imagined, to excuse what they have become.

My childhood was just about right. The times were lean, as times often are, but we had a loving family and the McCombs kids suffered no hardships. I don't know where it came from—neither of my parents were dreamers—but instead of obstacles I saw opportunity. This was instinctive to me.

When I was ten years old, I went into business for myself. (I don't know why it took me so long.) Somehow I had figured out one of the first rules of private enterprise. If you identify a need, and know where the buyers are, all that is missing is the product. I decided to sell roasted peanuts, for a nickel a bag, during the four weeks in winter that the migrant cotton pickers passed through Spur. If you have ever been to a ballpark, or on an airplane, you know that peanuts comprise one of the major food groups.

The workers normally came into our area in late November and early December. This was an annual pilgrimage. They would stay no more than a month, leaving the fields on Saturday and Sunday afternoons to visit Main Street, four blocks long. At the end of the street, certain ambitious townspeople would set up stands and sell homemade foodstuffs.

The idea of selling peanuts was inspired by the appearance of the Harley Sadler Medicine Show, which toured small towns peddling tonics and elixirs that would cure everything from baldness to lumbago. They put up a tent and staged a play, usually a melodrama, and peddled Cracker Jack and peanuts during the entertainment.

I didn't know where or how you bought quantities of Cracker Jack. But I found out that the Kimball wholesale grocery in Lubbock sold peanuts, and we had a delivery station in town. I went right over and asked the manager if they carried peanuts. He said, yes, in 100-pound sacks.

The next step was to ask my dad to be my banker. I explained that I was going to put the peanuts in brown paper bags and sell them to the cotton pickers. I knew, as children always do, that if I pestered him enough I would win. He knew it, too. But I don't believe Dad was displeased by my ambition. He had to quit school as a ten-year-old to work beside his father in a logging camp and help provide for his younger brothers and sisters. Eventually there would be eight of them.

I eagerly awaited the day when my load of peanuts would arrive on the truck from Lubbock. I worked early and stayed late, filling the brown bags, flipping them over with the ears on them. By the end of the week, I had sold my 100 pounds of goobers and had a mountain of nickels.

Proudly, I showed off my haul and took for granted that my dad would finance my next order. With his usual patience, he counted the nickels and said, slowly, "We have a little problem, honey boy. The peanuts cost more than you took in."

I was dumbfounded. But I learned a priceless lesson. I had a ready source of capital, my father. I had a labor source, meaning me. I had a market because I went right to the customers. What my business plan didn't include was figuring out how many bags I had to sell to make a profit.

Dad wasn't critical. He just said, "When you get the next hundred, cut the number of peanuts per bag in half. That way you'll double your money." That week, when I balanced my account, I had two mountains of nickels, one to pay off the peanuts and one to keep.

I did not see myself as a kid who was industrious in any special way. I mowed lawns, carried out groceries, picked up a dime here and a nickel there in tips. My first ongoing job was a paper route to deliver the *Lubbock Avalanche-Journal*. The boy who had been throwing the papers was moving to another town, and he offered to introduce me to the distributor.

From selling peanuts four weeks out of the year, I now took on a job that was as daily as it gets. There were two lessons learned, quickly and not painlessly. One, not everybody paid their bills. It was disheartening to throw the paper all week and not be able to collect. Two, people expected their paper whether it was snowing, sleeting, freezing, or storming.

My mother didn't want me delivering the papers—period. But, bless her, many of those freezing mornings when I would roll out of bed at 5:00 to ride my bicycle, she would get up to drive me instead. She would be angry about the hour, and the weather, and the inconvenience, but she insisted on taking me in the car. I never once asked her to do so. In fact, I dreaded it because she complained so incessantly.

One morning she commanded me, "Sit down. I have to talk to you. I want to know, why are you doing this? You don't need to do it. I do not enjoy getting up before dawn, in the bitter cold, but I am not going to let you go out on that ice, on a bicycle, and kill yourself. So tell me, why do you do this?"

She really could not understand my persistence. Her questions hinted that I was making my parents look bad. I didn't need the money. My dad had a job. He always had a job. My mother would shake her head and say, many times, "I gave birth to him and raised him, but I never have known what made that boy tick." To me, it was so obvious. This was a resource, a chance to have a job, to make my own money. I didn't analyze how I felt. It was just as natural as breathing.

When I was twelve, I had an opportunity to land a better job—riding the fender of a milk truck and jumping off to leave the customer's dairy order at the door. The job paid a little more than tossing papers, and was seven days a week, morning and night. I took home all the milk the family could use, and I didn't have to pump that bicycle up hills.

I looked around to see if I could find a buyer for my paper route. It's odd to look back over the years and see how, and when, we learn to value ourselves. I had paid nothing to the boy before me, but I had built up the route so that it turned a profit of three or four dollars a week. I just assumed that it was worth money.

The town had one general insurance agency and the owner had a son a year older than me. He wanted his son to have the job, and I offered to sell it to him for $50 cash. He didn't question the price; said it was fine. The day the distributor came down from Lubbock, the man asked him if the price was fair.

The distributor responded that the routes were not open to being sold. The newspaper decided who got them. I sensed that the distributor regretted having to say it. The father turned to me and said, "Well, Red, it looks like we can't pay you for the route."

I said, "Fine, but in that case I'm keeping it."

At that point, the distributor said, "Let's step outside for a minute." Once we were alone, he said, "I'm sorry I said that, but it's the truth. We can't allow you to sell your paper route, but I think I can fix this."

We went back inside. "Red can keep the route," he told the insurance agent. "He does a good job for us. But if you want it, give Red fifty dollars, not for the route, but to show your boy how to do it."

The son threw the papers for six months, then quit. The distributor wanted me to take it back, but I had moved on. I was riding the fender of that Model A Ford and bringing home all the milk my family could drink, plus cash.

Those were pastoral times in most of America. Families gathered around the radio at night and listened to Jack Benny, George Burns and Gracie Allen, Fred Allen, Eddie Cantor, the Lone Ranger, The Shadow, and a host of real and imagined legends. The movies gave us action and glamour: Tom Mix, Dick Powell, Greta Garbo, Shirley Temple, Mickey Mouse, King Kong, and *The Wizard of Oz*.

Franklin D. Roosevelt was the dominant political figure of that era, a landslide winner over Herbert Hoover in 1932 and Alf Landon in 1936. Roosevelt spoke to the nation in his fireside chats on radio, and his New Deal brought an alphabet soup of government agencies—the WPA, CCC, NYA, and others—in an effort to reduce unemployment and make the economy stable.

Prohibition was a failed idea that made drinking more desirable and more dangerous. The act was repealed in

1933, and two of the mobsters who had profited the most went down, too. Al Capone was sent to prison for income tax evasion, and John Dillinger was gunned down in front of a movie theater in Chicago.

Headlines of the 1930s were filled with news of the kidnapping of the Lindbergh baby, the abdication of the English throne by King Edward VIII for "the woman I love," and the explosion of the *Hindenburg*, the great German dirigible, over New Jersey.

When I was twelve, I moved to the job of washing dishes at a local cafe after school and on weekends. An elderly spinster, Mrs. Smith, owned and lived over the cafe, which seated about ten at the counter in addition to tables that seated four each. She would retire to take a nap when I got there after school.

The cook and waitress was a woman in her thirties named Evelyn, who had been divorced. In our town, in that period, a divorced woman carried a stigma. She was not considered a "good" person. Thirtyish and average-looking, Evelyn lived on a farm nearby and had little or no social life.

I liked her. She was helpful and considerate and taught me about short order cooking and how to make stews and *chile con carne*. She represented my first encounter with the abrupt and random turns of life and personal relationships.

One night, my second year at the cafe, less than an hour to closing time, a relatively new car pulled into a parking space. A man wearing a suit and a hat, a fellow unknown to me and to the town, walked in.

I watched through the service window as Evelyn went to the counter to wait on him. She drew him a cup of coffee, and I saw him reach inside his coat, pull out a pint of whiskey, and pour some into the cup. I just knew that God was going to send a lightning bolt through that cafe and strike us all dead.

As a twelve-year-old, my eyes opened up. Evelyn had gotten herself a cup of coffee and was leaning over the counter. The stranger poured some whiskey into her cup. I couldn't hear their conversation, but after a few sentences she walked back into the kitchen and I was literally petrified from what I had seen.

She untied her apron and wiggled into her coat. She said, "Red, when Mrs. Smith comes down to check the register, tell her I quit and not to worry about the three days' wages she owes me. I don't care. I'm giving it to you."

"Where are you going?" I asked.

"I don't know," said Evelyn, "but it will be better than where I am now." And a minute or two later, she walked out the door with a man she had never seen before.

With that Baptist church bell ringing in my ear, Mrs. Smith, in her high-necked collar, made her way down the stairs. "Where is Evelyn, Red?" she asked.

"She said to tell you she quit, Mrs. Smith," I blurted out.

"Well, where is she?"

"I don't know. She just left."

"What do you mean?"

"She just took off her apron and said to give the three days' wages she had coming to me. She was quitting and she wasn't coming back."

"What on earth prompted her to do that?" the old lady asked.

"I don't have any idea."

I thought a lot about what had happened. The man was traveling through town, probably heading west, and he saw a reasonably attractive woman. In the movies, this would have been Veronica Lake leaning over a formica counter, having a cup of java with a stranger. This was 1939; the depression was still a reality, jobs were short, money was scarce. I hope they grew to care about each other and stayed together a long time. But I doubt it turned out that way.

The story stirred a few days of gossip. The offshoot was that Mrs. Smith took Evelyn's place and showed me how to do the sandwich orders, so she could go upstairs and take her nap. The business wasn't much in the afternoon hours, and we usually closed around 8:00 or 8:30 P.M. I would be the cook, waiter, and cashier, with no increase in pay. At the outset, I'm sure she intended to hire a replacement for Evelyn. But as time went on, she saw I could handle it. We never had more than five or six people at a time. I had a repertoire that consisted of sandwiches, hamburgers, chili, and beef stew.

By 1940, I began to witness, and be a part of, one of the most profound changes that ever swept across America. This was when people began to leave the rural areas and went to what we called "war plants" as far away as California. Closer to home, the North American Aviation Company turned out airplanes on an assembly line, in Fort Worth.

The big news that started drifting back to Spur was: "Hey, not only did I land a job, but they gave my wife one and they are paying her as much as they are paying me." This struck me as unbelievable. When I was growing up, the only jobs women had were teaching school, nursing, and waitressing. Even the banks had male secretaries. There weren't many jobs for women outside the home.

The years 1940 and 1941, bringing with them an outbreak of global temper, are vivid to me to this day. I was struck by the enormity of the changes taking place, of people going off to what I perceived to be the outside world. And the women were getting decent employment.

With the Japanese bombing of Pearl Harbor on December 7, 1941, we were drawn into the war that had begun two years earlier in Europe. America was changed forever. I was so aware of the times, so fascinated by them. I was little different, I suppose, from most teenage boys on the threshold of becoming men, excited by this good war being waged against the forces of tyranny.

I had witnessed the mid-to-late 1930s, when hungry, jobless, defeated men, called hoboes, straggled through even our little town, which was not on a main route going west. I saw people who slept in our yard at night, wanting to work, knocking timidly at the door, asking, "Is there anything I can do to earn a meal?"

I saw my mother feed literally hundreds of them, up to 1939. Then it was pretty well over. Many times I saw entire families—men, women, children, aunts and uncles—and Mom feeding them whatever she could spare. I heard Dad say, "I wish I could do more," as he handed a man a dollar. Gasoline was a nickel a gallon, and this was money to get you up the road. We didn't have social services. It wasn't part of our world at the time. The depression left its stamp on my brain, and it will always be there.

When I was fifteen, and the war had scooped up most of the young men, I was able to leave the cafe and step up to the best job in town: working in the drug store. I owed this break to the wife of a doctor named Blackwell, who owned the pharmacy and let the druggist manage it. The Blackwells were considered "moneyed" folks. The doctor's wife was a gentle and pleasant person who befriended me in small ways and large.

She got me the job. I worked with an older boy, probably seventeen or eighteen, who had finished high school. I was a typical soda jerk, mopping the floors, stocking the shelves, keeping the syrup dispensers full at the fountain. I worked after school, and by summer I had hit the big-time, earning a dollar a day—seven dollars cash a week.

As a reference point, my father was making only $25 a week and raising a family.

Life was on a downhill pull. I was buying Arrow shirts—not many people could afford Arrow shirts back then. I played the French horn in the school band. On one memorable day we played as the first of Spur's young soldiers and sailors boarded the train to serve their country.

My hormones kicked in and I was doing pretty well in the girlfriend department. I gave them extra dips of ice cream and on the sly refilled their cherry Cokes.

By accident, I learned that the guy I was working with was making a buck and a half—ten dollars a week! This was my first lesson in negotiations, and it was a difficult one. After getting paid one Sunday night, I told the druggist that since I was doing the same work as Leon, and doing it well, I wanted to be paid the same money.

The druggist looked at me and said, "You do work as well as Leon. You have been a good employee," with the emphasis on HAVE. "Fact is," he went on, "I've been stretching things to keep you on and I enjoyed having you here. Good luck to you."

Uh-oh. I didn't think I had given him an ultimatum. In my mind, I had asked him for a raise, but I didn't tell him I was going to quit. I turned this over in my mind and concluded that I had made a major error. It was painfully clear that Mrs. Blackwell had leaned on him to give me the job and maybe he didn't really need me at all. I was truly upset. I had blown the best job (for a teenager) in Spur, Texas.

I couldn't wait for the sun to come up. As soon as it did, I jumped on my bicycle and hustled over to Mrs. Blackwell's house. I told her I was embarrassed and explained that the disaster of my life had taken place.

She very gently said, "Let me explain what probably happened here. You do the same job, you do it as well, but Leon is a full-time employee. You are part-time, even though you work full-time in the summer. So you were not necessarily wrong in what you did." She let me down beautifully. She said she would go back to the druggist and ask him to reconsider. He did, and I got the job back. Another huge lesson learned. And one of those moments that help shape your character.

I was still working at the drug store when my folks announced we were moving to Corpus Christi. There were virtually no parts left to fix cars with, and even though his employer, the Godfrey and Smart Ford Company, kept him on the payroll, Dad was eager to do something for the war effort. He took a leave of absence to work at the Corpus Christi Naval Station. It was incidental to him that the job paid four times what he made in the Ford service department. They wouldn't need him again until the war was won.

The rest of the family went to Corpus, but I stayed in Spur, moving into the house with Leon, whose family had gone west to get work in a defense plant. I used the excuse that I wanted to graduate with my high school class. That was partly true.

But I still had no intention of leaving Spur.

A turning point in my life, and possibly what is referred to today as a "defining moment," occurred when my mother knocked me out with a tennis racket. This was after my family moved to Corpus Christi during the war and I had talked her into letting me stay behind in Spur for an indefinite time.

I had a choice job at the City Drug, had discovered girls and vice versa, and was living about as well as I possibly could. My mom would call me once a week, to ask me when I planned to join them, and I kept stalling. The drug store really needed me, I assured her, at least until school reopened in the fall.

One afternoon in late August, I looked up from the soda fountain and saw my mother walk in, unannounced. We embraced and she invited me to dinner at a friend's house, where she was spending the night. I promised to be there right after we closed.

I had no guarded thoughts at all. I went sailing into the house and didn't even get all the way through the screen door when my mom confronted me. She had been to the place I had been boarding and collected all of my clothes and personal items. "It's all in the car," she said. "I packed us something to eat. We're going to drive at night because it's cooler."

At which time I made a nice little speech to the effect that I would not be leaving, now or never. My life was in Spur, Texas, and I would stay in touch.

She said, "I thought that was what you would say, Billy Joe," a name no one else called me. With that, she reached behind a chair and brought out the tennis racket, which happened to be my own. Tennis was considered a game for rich kids in the 1940s, and much later, but I enjoyed it. And, although not rich, I always had money.

I didn't have time to really channel these thoughts because Mom swatted me up the side of the head with the racket. I was addled, very addled, the way you are when you are knocked senseless, and I actually fell to my knees. She said she didn't want to hit me again, but I'd better get in that car. I believe she may have popped me one more time, but the first smash busted most of the strings.

I was mad and upset and didn't say three words on the trip to Corpus Christi, on the South Texas coast. My dad had taken a job at the Naval Air Base and rented a little place, temporarily, on North Beach. After I finished moping, I walked down to the water's edge. There I met a group of kids hanging out and, in fifteen minutes, I decided my whole world belonged in Corpus because I just hadn't realized there was anything else but Spur, Texas.

Best of all, I met and dated a beautiful girl named Charline Hamblin, fell in love, and knew I would marry her. I've always said that, from the day I realized I was a salesman, I have signed only one lifetime contract, and that was with Charline.

I never, ever returned to Spur but once, and that was in the late 1980s, when my brother Gene, by then a distinguished Baptist minister, living in Memphis, Tennessee, was preaching a sermon at the church. I flew Mom out there for the day.

It had been easy enough, I thought, to convince her to let me stay. That was my first experiment at making a quality of life decision. Like all parents, Mom was perceptive. She knew I wasn't going to come voluntarily, so she just elected to go fetch me.

My dad never swatted me or even raised a hand to me, and certainly not to my sisters, who adored him, or to Gene, who has probably led the purest life of anyone I have ever known.

Mother was free with the switch and the belt and rightfully so. She was the decisionmaker in the family. Dad was quite happy to let her make the calls. He was delighted, in fact. He worshiped her. Dad was a big man, at six-foot-three, with a sweet disposition. He and mother were both brunettes, who had two redheaded sons.

Mom's mother, my grandmother Dempsey, belonged to the Church of Christ, and to the most orthodox segment, which believed that if you belonged anywhere else you were going straight to hell. I can recall visiting Grandma Dempsey and hearing her say, "Gladys, are you still going to that Baptist church?"

My mom's response was, "Yes, I am, and I love it more every day." And without raising her voice, my grandmother would say, "You're going to hell, Gladys. I'm sorry, but you're going to hell."

As a kid, I thought, how can this be? My mother was always the one who was right. And in the end, I have to say she usually was.

There was a slight contradiction in my father's family. While Dad was a dedicated churchgoer, he and his kin were Scot-Irish and not opposed to drinking. They were not drunkards by any stretch of the imagination. But, like a lot of backwoods people and dirt farmers, when they had access to liquor they would drink until nothing was left. Then they would pass out and sleep it off. I never saw any of them do anything violent or even disorderly.

But my mother hated liquor. If anyone in Dad's family, including Dad, came to the door with alcohol on his breath, she would not let him in the house. My father had to visit in the yard.

One time we were going to a picnic at a place called Roaring Springs. One of the old cars had a blowout, and when the men got into the well to retrieve the spare tire, my mother spotted two bottles of whiskey that had been placed there by Dad's brothers, or perhaps his father. Mom busted the two bottles on the hub in one fell swoop, and all they could do was stand there. My dad never said a word. Mother absolutely detested liquor. She said many times over, "I would rather see any one of you children in a coffin than with a glass of whiskey in your hand."

So, even as I grew up and got into my social drinking days, and beyond, I never drank in front of my mother nor served any liquor around her.

Another defining moment for me as a young man really evolved over a period of years.

Growing up in Spur, I made a crucial discovery. The three people in town who seemed to be involved in all the decisionmaking were the banker, the lawyer, and the doctor. In my narrow world, I made no distinction between state issues and national issues. Wherever I lived, I was fascinated by those who were in charge. I thought about it for hours on end: how do you get to be one of those elite few? I wanted to be in that role.

I didn't do well in science, so I figured that ruled out my becoming a doctor. I didn't have a clue about what kind of education you needed to be a banker, or what path you took, so I scratched that one. It seemed clear to me that if I was going to achieve my goal, I had to make it as a lawyer.

This is the short version of how I changed directions (more later):

I attended Southwestern University, in Georgetown, Texas, on a football scholarship, even though I knew I was not much more than mediocre as an athlete. I never forgot that and, a lot of years later, I served as chairman of the school's board of trustees, helped the school raise $95 million, and donated some of my own. I believe that when you can afford it, you need to give something back to the people and places that put you on the right path.

I wanted as much formal education as I could get, as long as it didn't slow me down. I enrolled at the University of Texas business school and then the law school, and enjoyed both. I was your basic B student, with an attitude. I always thought you had to decide where to put your energies. I had been an entrepeneur from the time I was ten. I enjoyed college life, but I felt the extra hours that were required to be a better student could be put to better use elsewhere.

Late in the fall semester of my second year, in UT Law School, one of my fraternity brothers, who had graduated, dropped by and stayed for supper. He had ranked in the top five percent of his class and had helped me with some courses as a tutor. I was shocked to find out that he had come back to school to earn some extra hours working on campus and doing some practice teaching. The reason he had returned was that, in 1950, the range of pay offered to the top graduates was $350 to $375 a month.

Of course, this was before we had become such a litigious society. But I knew I was not by any definition a top student, so where did this leave me? I went over to the law school and confided my misgivings to one of the deans. He gave me a royal ass-chewing. He said that the best lawyers did not enter the field to make money, but because it was an honorable profession. One did not expect to make "big" money until one had labored for years—at least.

I left his office in shock. I wanted to be a lawyer so I could be one of the select few who made the wheels turn. For advice, I talked to an economics professor I admired. I mentioned that I might drop out of school. He understood my concern. He told me that if I wanted to make money, I ought to get in the selling business.

"Like what?" I asked.

"Oh, high-ticket items," he replied. "Commissions won't have to wait until you learn all the ropes. You get paid on production."

Within a couple of weeks, I had lined up a job in Mississippi with a Texas ex who was selling heavy equipment to build highways, roads, and dams. I would be paid primarily on commission, with a small salary.

I finished the fall semester, took my last final, and drove down to Corpus Christi, where my parents were living. Fate, and Mama, must have known what they were doing when they dragged me out of Spur. If they hadn't, I might never have met Charline.

One night, after a date, I dropped by a joint where some of my friends liked to hang out. One of them asked what I was doing at home and I told him I had a new job that started in six weeks. He asked why I would want to do that. He was a salesman at a Ford dealership and suggested that I should try it. That was the last thing I wanted. My father was a mechanic most of his life, and proud to be one, the best I ever saw at diagnosing a problem and fixing it. But as a kid, I hadn't seen anything attractive about the car business. I saw long hours and low pay.

Then my friend said, "You're going to work the oil fields down south, pull iron and live on the ground with the snakes. Charline is here. We don't have to work hard. We spend half the day shooting pool. And they give us a new car to drive."

When he told me what he was making, it didn't take me long to do the math. I said, "That's as much as I'll make working doubles," which meant sixteen hours a day.

He lifted his glass. "Come on down. I'll introduce you to the sales manager."

Right off the bat, I knew this was something I enjoyed.

Cars were easy to sell. That hasn't changed. Within three weeks, I knew this was something I wanted to do. I looked at the structure. I got acquainted with the business manager, who let me look at the operating statements. The business manager was impressed that a car salesman had shown an interest in accounting.

I slipped around and got acquainted with the parts manager and found out what his role was. Whatever entry level you took—parts, sales, service or accounting, any of the four—you were only about three steps from the bottom to the top. I found it to be an interesting business. Look out, I thought—I could be a dealer in a year!

In 1950 the national sales average was more or less ten units per month. That is still the national average today. I had no training, but they put me with another salesman and I looked at the procedures and the paperwork. After three weeks of really getting involved, I set for myself a goal of one car a day. I sold thirty-one cars a month for three years, and I still have all my pay slips to this day because I was proud of them.

That was a wild, wonderful, wacky, and confusing year, 1950. It was the time of Senator Joe McCarthy and the Communist menace. I kept seeing bumper stickers that said, "Better Dead Than Red."

CHAPTER 2

HEART LIKE A WHEEL

Contrary to popular belief, the greatest love story of the twentieth century was not the Duke and Duchess of Windsor, Gable and Lombard, Bogey and Bacall, or even Donald Trump and himself.

The romance that never ends is the one between the American people and the automobile. Part of it has to do with our obsession with speed and power and the call of the open road. The rest is marketing.

Anyone who ever passed a truckload of hay on the highway can imagine, for the moment, how it might feel to be an A. J. Foyt or a Jeff Gordon. But I try not to get caught up in the symbolism of the car. Never have. Nor in the size, design, style, or price. Those decisions are made by the manufacturer. I have nothing to do with them. So I put my ideas and energy where they counted. I was a car peddler.

In my first year of selling cars, I had some novel concepts. But because I was twenty-two, my ideas were not welcome. Like every other dealership in 1950, we were perpetuating the myth of a postwar car shortage. In a given week, as few as fifteen cars would be available for sale, even though seventy-five were being stored in a warehouse.

I told my bosses, "Hey, why not pull out those cars we're hiding and hold a major sale?" They just stared at me. From then on, I encouraged young people to speak their minds if they thought they knew a better way.

By the end of the year, I had been recognized as the top salesman in town, but still I was too young to get a job in management. That didn't dampen my ambitions. There were other chances to make money, and I jumped on them. I got my license to sell car insurance. And if a person called to ask if I sold residential insurance, I said, "Sure, I can take care of that." I would turn it over to a real estate agent and take a commission.

I met a builder who was doing one or two homes at a time. I asked him why he didn't do three or four. We went to a bank, set up a line of credit, and became partners in building houses. I made a little money out of that.

My world was good. Charline and I were married in 1950. Our first of three daughters, Lynda Gay McCombs, was born on December 29, 1951. I got involved with the Chamber of Commerce. But I was itching to take the next step. Our dealership had good, solid management and no openings, so I contacted some of the others. The response was the same. I was still too young.

Didn't they realize that Alexander the Great was twenty-four when he conquered the world?

By 1953, with three years of selling behind me, I decided I had to go out on my own. I made an appointment with a local banker, Eugene Dabney of the Corpus Christi Bank and Trust. I spread my business plan across his desk. My request was for a $12,500 loan to open a used car lot. I would finance all my contracts with the bank and let them keep the reserve. I planned to sell my house — I had saved about $7,000 — and that money would go into the deal.

Mr. Dabney looked at the plan and after a long, stony silence, said, "That is the silliest thing I ever heard of. You can throw that in the trash."

I said, "What don't you like?"

"I don't like any of it," he replied. "You're twenty-five years old. You got a new house, a wife, and a baby. You're working for the best car company in town. What else do you want?"

"I want my own business," I said. Damn, what could be simpler? I straightened up the papers and continued, "Let's go through this again. You have always been supportive of me and I'm grateful for your advice. You are the smartest banker in town."

Actually, he had never done anything for me.

Mr. Dabney didn't try to conceal his disbelief. "You don't show that you're taking down any of the finance reserve."

"I'm not. I'm going to let the bank apply it to my debt."

"You haven't made any provision for taxes," he added.

"Yes, I have."

"Well, you can't operate without keeping the reserve. It can't be done."

"Yes, it can, because I will do everything myself—buy, sell, finance, and keep the books. And if I don't succeed, I'll pay you back every dime and admit the plan failed. But there is one thing I can always do. I can sell cars."

He was a stereotype of what we used to think bankers should look like—a bald, cigar-smoking, dour man. I wore him down. "This is the silliest thing I've ever done," he said. "I'm going to do it, but I will be keeping a close watch on you."

I quit my job at the Ford dealership and left with the

blessings of Austin Hemphill, the kindly gentleman who was my first boss. I would never have another.

McCombs Used Cars started out with two salesmen, including myself. I would buy cars out of town and drive them back to Corpus. To Mr. Dabney's surprise, and relief, I quickly paid off our loan and opened a second lot. Both prospered. It was a fun time, and very rewarding.

In 1957, Ford Motor Company was coming out with the first totally new car since World War II, and the most expensive new product launch in history. It was to be called the Edsel.

With the help of Austin Hemphill, I was granted the Edsel franchise in Corpus Christi. I was the youngest dealer in the country, and I could not have been more proud or excited—right up to the moment when I realized the car wouldn't sell.

I knew it within a month. It had taken the company five years to bring this vision to the marketplace, and it had endured a good bit of infighting in Detroit. Robert McNamara, who would become the first person outside the family to run the company, kept his distance from it. He followed the same philosophy at Ford as he later did as secretary of defense: "There is no strategy. There is only crisis management."

The Edsel had no advantage in price or new options and a design that drew puzzled reviews. What it had was a grill that people compared to a horse collar, or worse.

The car went on sale the first week of September 1957. Given the early hype and the public's curiosity, the initial reaction was promising. I had the four best salesmen in Corpus working with me and, at the start, we averaged fifty to sixty-five sales a month. The people who looked it over were overwhelmed. We made a little money.

Even so, within a month I notified Ford the car wouldn't sell. As the weeks went by, it became too exhausting an effort to close the sale. There was too much resistance. The dogs didn't like the dog food.

At the factory, they thought I was way out in left field. Why was I being so negative, they asked, when I was supposed to be pushing this car? I was selling more Edsels than any dealer in Texas and making a profit. And that was why. I didn't want to wrestle every customer to get them behind the wheel.

I was an Edsel dealer for exactly five months. My friend Austin Hemphill, who had moved to San Antonio, warned me I was being too hasty by bailing out. My banker urged me not to be too quick on the trigger. "Stay the course," he said. "You're young. Be patient."

Much more personal, and more difficult, was the knowledge that my father disapproved. Over the years, he questioned some of my decisions in depth, but never in anger. I was frequently critical of the product, the style and design of the cars, and this made him defensive. To him, Ford Motors could do no wrong, and he never liked to hear me criticize the company.

This was that basic loyalty that had been a part of his life since he walked off the farm at nineteen. It was part of the character of a man who never sought glory, recognition, or monetary gain for himself. I saw him cry only twice in his life: when Henry Ford died, and when FDR died.

His basic thought on the Edsel was: I should have stayed with it for as long as the company did because the Ford Motor Company would make it work.

At the time, no one lined up to tell me I was making the right decision. But I never hesitated. The Edsel was simply not going to be a success, and I would not let it undo what I had just begun to build. I still had my two car lots and added a leasing facility, buying used equipment. Lost no money at all.

Four years to the month after it was launched, Ford announced that the Edsel was being discontinued. It had cost $350 million to develop. The company stock dropped 20 points.

It was a sad day. The car had been named as a tribute to Henry Ford's only son, born in 1893 and dead of cancer at the age of forty-nine. As Bill Ford, one of Edsel's three boys, put it, you can't be pleased when your father's name becomes a synonym for failure.

In December of that year, when Austin Hemphill realized I was out of the Edsel, he invited me to his new home in San Antonio. I loved him like a father, and when I got to the house we drank a lot of Scotch while I analyzed his operating statement. It showed that he was nearly broke.

He had built a new dealership a year or so earlier and now was on the verge of being wiped out. The country had slipped into a recession. The Ford lineup in '58 was a dud and sales were off everywhere. Bottom line: he was overdrawn at the bank, and had covered it, as many car dealers do, by what is called an out-of-trust maneuver. The dealer signs a trust agreement when he gets the title. He is obligated to pay off the lender, but he can float that for as much as sixty days because, obviously, he isn't audited by the hour. It isn't unlike the common household practice of writing checks to pay your bills, and hoping your deposit beats them to the bank.

In Austin's case, he was overdrawn by $100,000, and his inventory was being audited even as we spoke. He was a lawyer and understood the consequences. "If I don't get this deal turned around," he said, "I'm busted. Do you have any thoughts?"

I was stunned. "The first thing we do," I said, "is cure the out-of-trust."

"We can't," he said. "I don't have the money."

I said, "I do and I'll loan it to the company. I don't know how else I can help, but I'll be back in January to try." I had no strategy, but I was learning fast about crisis management. I figured I would spend four weeks, tops, devote all my effort to the dealership, and see if I could salvage it. To be honest, I had no idea if I could help or not.

After we butchered that bottle of Scotch, and talked for hours, I drove back to Corpus Christi.

If I could avoid it, I tried not to spend a full night away from home. It was late when I pulled into the driveway, still reeking of alcohol. As I eased into bed to kiss my beautiful wife, I said, "Honey, this is going to be hard for you to believe, and I'll explain it in the morning, but we're going to have to spend some time in San Antonio."

Half-awake, Charline patted me over her shoulder and said, "Honey, go to sleep. You'll feel better in the morning."

It was a quarter of 3:00 in the morning. Sinatra time.

On the 2nd of January, I got up at 4:00 A.M. to drive to San Antonio. At 8:30, I walked into a meeting with Mr. Hemphill and his management team and sales force. He said, in effect, "All of you know about our problems. This is Red McCombs. I have a lot of confidence in him. Whatever he says, it is just the same as my saying it." In short, he gave me full authority over the dealership. After the meeting broke up, he put his arms around me, gave me a hug, and said, "If you need me, call the house." With that he got into his car and drove home.

This was my introduction to a big-time operation. In Corpus, I had five employees on two lots and did all the title applications, kept the books myself, and more. Hemphill had sixteen salesmen. I told them I would talk to each one individually.

I had these talks, off and on, all day. I laid out my plan, which was that we would operate just as I had with my used car lots. By 3:00 P.M., the sales force had reduced itself to five. The others just walked out.

The five who stayed were invaluable to me, and they were rewarded later when I was able to help them get their own dealerships. They all became successful dealers.

I was disappointed that the others had left. Realizing that I was plowing new ground, after getting over the initial shock of Mr. Hemphill's speech, I sat down at his desk and wondered what I was doing there. I felt sick to my stomach, nauseated. I actually threw up in a wastebasket in the office. I excused myself from the dealership and drove aimlessly for an hour, trying to clear my head.

By the time I pulled back into the parking lot, I realized that I had a real opportunity to help a friend. Here was a man who had turned his only asset over to me to do with as I thought best. No compliment of that magnitude had ever come my way. So I went from feeling sick to being exhilarated. All a matter of attitude.

I got together with the five salesmen who were left and told them we were going to do things that were beyond their imagination. All we had to do was stay together. Our comeback would start with me talking to every single person who walked into that dealership or called on the phone.

In car dealerships, you have two invisible partners who are absolutely essential to your success. One is the manufacturer who supplies the product; in this case, Ford. The other is your bank or finance company.

In the auto industry, the reality is that we operate under the dumbest law any business ever imposed upon itself. In their unbelievably brainless judgment, the auto dealers lobbied Congress for years to get what we know today as the Sticker Law. The federal government mandated that the manufacturer must put the retail price on the sticker of the car, and for good measure they have always set the wholesale price to the dealer.

This is the only business I know where the factory picks the prices, both wholesale and retail.

You can see quickly what happened to the margins in the largest retail business in America. Meanwhile, the dealer has no say as to how the product will be designed or priced.

What bugged me most of all was that dealers were so

proud of the system. Years of lobbying and multimillions of dollars had gone into this effort. Auto dealerships soaked up capital, not only for the inventory but to purchase the contracts of their customers. In 1958, Ford Motor did not yet have a credit corporation (this came into being in the early 1960s). So the dealers had to arrange their financing through other sources.

Just as I had done with my used car lots, I offered a Buy Here/Pay Here program, with coupon booklets and payment notices, and secured a guaranteed line of credit at the bank.

The next problem I encountered was the simple fact that the 1958 model Ford was what the industry politely called a dog. It had no appeal to the customer whatsoever. This happens to the best of them from time to time, but since my role was to help my friend, we had to find a way to make the public think the line was attractive. The '58 Ford was the only baby I had.

This leap would require marketing and advertising, and I had not been much involved with either. But I got lucky. I have been blessed all through my career, many ways, many times. This was one of them.

The challenge was to make the public like a car it had little reason to like. Looking at the resources we had to spend, I decided essentially to put all of my money with one source—for a period of two weeks.

I had never met a local radio rock and roll disc jockey named Ricci Ware, but I knew he had the hottest morning show in San Antonio. So I had to figure out a way to contact him. People who know me today might find this statement somewhat curious, but I had no identity in San Antonio—period. I was riding through the desert on a horse with no name.

For me to call the station, KTSA, to talk to the hottest jock on the air, whose ego was even bigger than his reputation, required some thought on my part. How was I going to gain access? I decided not to be cute. I called, identified myself as a new Ford dealer in town, and asked to speak to Ricci Ware. I was told I wanted to talk to a sales executive. I said, "No, this is a personal matter and I have some information Mr. Ware needs. So have him call me."

A puzzled and haughty Ricci Ware returned my call, and virtually his first words were, "I never heard of you."

In that one phone call, I told him I had a grand plan and I needed him to help me. I had chosen him and only him for what I had in mind. Within an hour he was sitting in my office.

I told him why I was there, what my role was, to help a friend through a distressful time. I would give him my entire budget for two weeks to see if he could put people in our showroom. In addition to the regular spots, I would be using, in effect, his popularity and acceptance. I would actually own his show. He would be talking about the new gang at Hemphill Ford and would put his own personality into delivering much more than just a commercial.

If he had any integrity at all, I could not offer him anything under the table to do this. I soon learned that he had as much integrity as any man I ever knew, and to this day I consider Ricci and his wife Mimi and their children part of my family. So I appealed to his ego and the humble nature that he hid under the surface, to help someone in trouble. Ricci bought into it. He delivered people to our dealership in big numbers, and we kick-started our sales campaign with that one concept.

We sold all our cars, and the key was logic and common sense. I didn't need 50,000 people in there. I just needed fifteen or twenty a day. So why not concentrate my money in one place? I not only did this with Ricci and KTSA, but I could now afford to go to the other station and cut a similar deal.

My next stop, more or less, was at the office of my new financial partner, Dwight Weir, the manager for the UCIT

Corporation, who floor-planned the cars and bought the notes from the customers. I explained to Mr. Weir that the company was overdrawn by $100,000.

He wrinkled up his nose in a way that pushed his glasses above his eyebrows. His bald head even had wrinkles. He said, "I've never seen you before. Who are you and what are you after?"

I said, "I'm after your help." I was totally honest with him, then added, cheerfully, "Why don't we get a drink?" I had been told he enjoyed a drink occasionally.

He said, "It may take more than one drink if you're over here telling me that my biggest account is broke and you're running the company for him."

I told him that was about the size of it.

My plan had been to not spend more than four weeks in San Antonio. I knew I had to have Mr. Weir's support. In essence, although we did not buy the contracts, I put my initials on every one. While there would be no official guarantee, whether the customer paid or did not, on a handshake I agreed to buy back any car they were stuck with, and resell it in Corpus.

Honesty demands that I admit this was a gutsy call on my part, and a questionable management call on his part. But it made both of us very successful. We turned Hemphill Ford around in one week. Mr. Weir and his company were doing very well, and I was no longer initialing contracts.

I sold my two used car lots and made arrangements for Charline and our three little daughters to move to San Antonio in April of 1958. We had no way of knowing it was the move of a lifetime.

CHAPTER 3

IN THE DRIVER'S SEAT

In 1958, an off year, Austin Hemphill's floundering Ford dealership had 50 percent of the San Antonio market. Three other dealers were splitting the other half. As for the red-haired stranger, I was now a certified 90-day Wonder.

After three months, the managers at Ford Motor Company wanted me to fly to Detroit and talk about putting on sales meetings for them. I felt that I was in a fairly good bargaining position, and since I still had twenty-seven new Edsels I offered a swap: if the Edsel division would buy back my stock, I would go to California and do their sales meetings.

After all, what is car dealing if not horse trading?

Attitude is absolutely the most critical element in selling anything to all of America. You can't fake attitude. You either have it or you don't. I'm an open book. I don't usually have to explain myself because people know instantly what my feelings are. If I'm not positive, they can tell. If

I'm angry, even my dog can tell. And dogs are not unlike people in this respect: they know the difference between being kicked or stepped on accidentally. If your attitude is poor, change it. Go bust a tree stump or puke or whatever it takes. My spirits were soaring in 1958 because we had pulled one out of a ditch. Now Ford wanted me to tell my story. It was a good one to tell.

We restructured the company with Hemphill and McCombs as partners, 50-50. Austin offered me all of it, which he had no obligation to do, and I had too much conscience to accept.

In August of 1958, Ford contacted us about salvaging a dealership that was dropping like a marble down a drainpipe in Houston. It had lost money for twenty-two straight months. The location was wrong, the showroom was dilapidated, and the roof leaked. If it rained, they needed buckets on the floor. The guys in the service department had to roll up their pants because the garage flooded.

The good news was that they didn't need to worry about having to keep a lot of cars dry. They only had three in the showroom.

Mr. Hemphill and I met with the seller in Houston at the Shamrock Hotel. Normally, we would have been buying assets, but all they had were $2 million in losses. I looked at the balance sheet and, in a torrent of faith, figured we could carry that loss forward if we ever made big money. We needed to buy this company, warts and all. It was going to take $150,000 to bring it out of trust. I decided we would pay $300 for their stock, 300 shares of it. They were like mice that no longer wanted the cheese—they just wanted out of the trap.

We had done something in San Antonio that was unique to the industry. I leased four lots around the city, where we put both new and used cars. I persuaded Lee Iacocca to sign off on it as a test market. If it worked, to make it fair, other dealers could do the same. But the other dealers thought we were crazy.

My plan for Houston was five locations, four outdoors, with almost no overhead. Everyone who managed one of our lots ultimately became a dealer and wealthy in his own right.

All I heard was how the idea didn't have any hope. People kept reminding me of how little I knew about the city of Houston. But I could look past the Shamrock, toward Main Street and Fannin, and they were building the Texas Medical Center, one of the great facilities in the world. I saw some vacant land nearby, went to the owner, and convinced him to let me use it. I would get out in 120 days if he wanted, but in the meantime I promised to bring so much attention to that location he would have no trouble selling it.

He agreed to the deal. If he sold the property in that period of time, I would recover half the money I planned to spend on pavement and lights. But if I was there for three years, he would owe me nothing.

This was where I intended to capture the Houston market. I strung up hundreds of lights and put three trailers together as offices. I had one problem: Houston wasn't yet in a building boom, and I couldn't get power to my lights. I called Stewart and Stephenson, the oil field supply company, and asked to borrow a gas generator. I remembered this power source from my summer jobs as an oil rigger.

Eventually, the city complained because I wasn't buying electricity from them.

Car dealers can't operate in this fashion today and, in truth, they were not allowed to do it back then. Iacocca said many times that Red McCombs had a longer tenure with test programs than anyone in the history of Ford Motors.

I made another trail-blazing decision in Houston. I decided to use television and to put all my budget on only one of the city's three stations. I had their sales managers assemble in my suite at the Shamrock, asked for their proposals, and told them I would commit my money to one station.

After they left, I threw away their rate cards. Half an hour later, they began calling back. This was the deal: I would pay the 2:00 A.M. rate, but under the table I would be guaranteed half my spots in prime time. I took a six-month option and then signed up for six more. We broke the Houston market wide open in the second month, and that little bankrupt dealership became the most profitable in the city. It is still operated today by my friend and long-time partner, Charlie Thomas, the former owner of the Houston Rockets. Which is another story.

Now, to go on television with all these spots, I had to have a hook. My Christmas lights, strung across a full block, out by the Shamrock, were candy for the eye, but what was my sales hook? Anyone can say, "We have lower prices" or "We'll beat any deal." My hook was: "Two to one, the Ford in front of you came from Hemphill." The advertising people said I could not do it: I was not outselling my rivals by two-to-one. But that was not my claim. All I did was quote what the odds were. The slogan caught on. Newspaper columnists even wrote about looking at the Ford in front of them and not seeing a Hemphill sticker.

You couldn't buy publicity like that.

One other point came into play. Being able to make $2 million, and writing off the taxes, gave our little company the capital we needed. The return from that dealership was the basis of everything we have done since. I never calculated the total returns, but it was worth tens of millions to me and the same to Charlie Thomas.

Within a year we were in Dallas, but with a story not so successful. I had become a big name in auto circles in a year and a half. Ford asked me to jump into the Dallas market and take over a dealership that had been busted on Cedar Springs Avenue.

Ford was eager to get together with the other dealers and talk about how we were going to work together. That was a laugh. I had breakfast with five dealers and they told me, in no uncertain terms, that I had taken San Antonio and Houston by surprise. It would not happen in Dallas. They would lose money if necessary. This was not exactly the loving embrace you would hope to get from your new neighbors, but I thought we could overcome their hostility. I stayed eighteen months, made a little money, then called the other dealers and said, "You guys were right. I'm out of here."

But secretly, I had developed a marketing strategy for Dallas, one of the best of my career. I had found a three-story building on Cedar Springs, an old-timey building that used an elevator to bring up the cars. The building had no signage on it. At first I thought I could use the technique from Houston, but the lights wouldn't be as effective. Ford had an assembly plant in Dallas and had agreed to build me up to 1,500 cars in sequence, different models of Ford. I sat in my hotel room, trying to figure out what my promotion was going to be.

Then it came to me: FORD—factory direct to you. A convoy of trucks with these new cars, unloading at the warehouse on Cedar Springs, while photographers snapped pictures. And no name on the dealership.

Today that would be illegal. You have to identify yourself. But it wasn't illegal in July of 1959—just a little outrageous. I knew that not only would the other dealers rise up in arms, but Ford would come unglued. I kept it under wraps until the day we ran with it: big signs that shouted, "FORD — FACTORY DIRECT TO YOU."

We needed cops to take care of the traffic jams. I had to fly in salesmen from Houston and San Antonio. And I knew the heat was going to be unbelievable.

I hid out in a little motel not far from the site. The flack from the other dealers and Ford was intense. It got to a point where I even had to tell my partner, Austin Hemphill, that I "was not available."

Ford fired off a threatening message: "If we can't find

Red to stop this, we will have to get a court order to shut him down."

In five days we sold 600 cars. I never sold that many in that short a time, before or since—and I am not certain anyone else has.

When I finally emerged from the motel, like a mole from a tunnel, I apologized to everyone concerned. It was the least I could do. I explained that I didn't realize we were going to create that big a problem. I put my signs away and promised to play nice.

There is a certain amount of recklessness and courage that comes with youth. And, if I might add, a huge dose of sheer fun and mischief. Forty years later, I wish I could say the same thing, but I doubt that the young have the same kind of fearlessness as we did in the 1950s, when we had so little to lose.

I was now operating three franchise dealerships. When I moved to San Antonio, I had five employees back in Corpus Christi. I had a lot of learning to do, and I have never been shy about asking for help, or giving some.

I believe one of my assets is that I have no fear of losing. And no fear of people. By and large, I like them. I am not in awe of anyone I ever met, but I try to feel total respect for everyone, with the possible exception of the guy who designed the Edsel.

CHAPTER 4

ALL IN THE FAMILY

During my first fifteen years in the car industry, the three most influential men in my life were Henry Ford II, Lee Iacocca, and Willie Nathan McCombs. Of the three, my father may have been the most devoted to the Ford Motor Company and the one who cared the least about the money.

Young Henry suffered from being in the giant shadow of his grandfather, whose name he bore. Anyone would have. Old Henry had hand-built his first car in 1896, inspiring Will Rogers to later observe: "It will take a hundred years to tell whether he helped us or hurt us, but he certainly didn't leave us where he found us."

That verdict had been in long before I arrived. Just as I always wanted to be involved in the decisionmaking in the towns where I lived, I lobbied and politicked my way onto the Ford Dealer Council. Every manufacturer has one. I was elected chairman of the national council in 1963, five years after I became a Ford dealer. At that level, you have access to the company's leadership, including Henry the Second. I know, it sounds like royalty, but in a sense the Ford family was.

A national chair really represented 6,000 Ford dealers around the country in expressing their views and complaints and problems. In this position, I had contacts on an ongoing basis with Lee Iacocca. I found him to be everything that has been written of him: bright, extremely energetic, forceful, fun, and tough. We fought and laughed and had lots of battles. Obviously, Lee won most of them because he was the boss, the man who promoted the Mustang and revived the Ford racing team. The eighteen-hour workday was routine for him. He had a sort of Sicilian loyalty to his people and his ideas, but this did not include Henry the Second.

From time to time, certain issues went all the way to Henry's desk, and I loved the opportunity to push a program from the dealers' point of view, to act as their spokesman. Henry was totally aware of the goings-on in the company; he was very much hands-on. He did not mind giving you one of two answers, a "no" or a "hell no."

The items that came into question were the warranty, pricing, and options the competition had that we did not have—the whole gamut of a dealer's wish list. The relationship with the manufacturer was one that people outside the business had a hard time understanding. There was distrust and animosity, where you would expect an atmosphere more akin to Santa Claus and his elves.

Before Ross Perot sold his General Motors shares back to the company, he called one day from Dallas and asked if he could fly down and spend a couple of hours with me on what he called the "automotive" business. He wanted to know why this chasm existed, why everyone was not on the same page, why the lack of respect was so jarring.

We had a lively discussion. The question that nagged

at him was how to change this culture, how to fix it. I told him honestly that I didn't think anyone could. Publicly, we would say great things about each other. The car companies always stressed that they loved the dealers and how strong an asset they were. But the fact is, the contentious atmosphere that generally exists is part of the structure. You learn to live with it, which requires a lot of give and take by both sides.

Lee Iacocca was a down-to-earth, although very sophisticated, man, always ready to discuss the issues, to go head-to-head. He was at times sympathetic to our needs, although this rarely led to any positive results. Still, I didn't expect to have as much access as I did to the man who headed the Ford Division, a take-no-prisoners kind of guy.

What sticks out in my mind is how competitive Lee was. He absolutely had to win. He had a down-in-the-trenches mentality, a quality that appealed to a dealer. I had seen firsthand the clash of management styles when a disagreement existed between Mr. Ford, Lee, and myself.

One example involved the planning of the 1968 HemisFair in San Antonio. Our requirements included some twenty-six industrial exhibits and free-standing buildings that featured a theme. Such a commitment was expensive for any corporation, but for personal as well as marketing reasons I thought we could count on Ford.

We had three major companies on board, but then we hit a wall. My impassioned appeal to Ford had gone nowhere. At that point, the governor, John Connally, asked if I would take a review with the HemisFair staff and see if we could break the impasse.

The bottom line was that in San Antonio, a city loved by tourists but with a low per capita income, we had absolutely no entrée to corporate America. The morning I was to give my report to the governor, I was on the phone with Iacocca, begging Ford to commit to putting up a building. I reminded him that the proposal had been under consideration for a year. He replied flatly that the company was not going to do it. The conversation actually escalated into a cussing fight on the phone.

He said, "This fair has no economic or *political* significance for the Ford Motor Company." I remember just boiling when he referred to "that dusty little town" of ours, concluding with, "Mr. Ford will be sending a personal emissary to Governor Connally to select an art object as our gift."

I knew when I hung up with him, however, that our problem was solved. John Connally was one of my heroes, a handsome, imposing figure who turned heads when he walked into a room. He was then the most popular governor Texas ever had, respected across party lines, a man who carried the scars of wounds sustained in the car with President Kennedy.

When he answered my phone call, I said lightly, "Have I been stupid or what? Ford Motors doesn't see any economic or political significance to the HemisFair." Of course, the man in the White House was Lyndon Johnson, of Texas.

Connally said, "You call Iacocca and tell him we won't be bothering him again. The president will be calling Mr. Ford to point out what this fair means to the southwest and to the countries of the Western Hemisphere."

When I repeated these words to Lee, I could hear the sudden change of interest in his voice. He did not want us to go over his head. But the last thing he wanted was for Lyndon Johnson to negotiate directly with Henry. "Give me forty-eight hours," he said, "and let me talk to Governor Connally and see what we can work out."

The record will show that when the HemisFair opened, the governor and Lee Iacocca posed cheerfully for photographers in front of the grand, modern Ford Building.

Once we recognized what the key was, President Johnson made a call to other corporate heads, and our problems vanished. The HemisFair was a huge commercial and artistic success and literally put San Antonio on the international map. Many of the buildings were designed for later uses, including a convention center and arena that provided a big league home for the basketball Spurs.

Inevitably, Lee Iacocca and Henry Ford II parted company in the only way they could, with Henry the Second firing the confrontational Lee in 1976. Iacocca went on to become president of Chrysler. He took the company through bankruptcy and a federal bailout and in time would return it to prosperity. A year later, Henry stepped down as president, and in 1980 he resigned as chairman of the board, leaving the loyal and able Phil Caldwell to run the company.

For the first time in its history, there was no member of the Ford family running the Ford Motor Company.

The intrigue at corporate headquarters had no direct impact on what was transpiring in San Antonio, or Texas, but I had my own quota of missed opportunities. I am not one who feels tempted to look back and say what I wished I had done or not done. But I will think about what I could have done bigger and what I could have done better.

Ford had invited me, actually urged me, to enter the California markets at the start of the '60s, offering Phoenix, Las Vegas, and Albuquerque as well. I declined, and those were all big-time mistakes. I didn't think I would have the ability or the capital to succeed out west; I now know I would have.

I am generally credited with being a far thinker in this business, but I must admit there are serious indications that I was not. I did not understand that a small, odd-looking German car, the Volkswagen, would ever sell in the United States. I was wined and dined and courted, and offered the VW franchises for Houston. I politely said thanks but no thanks. Oops, again.

As Japanese cars began to roll onto our docks, I had major doubts that Americans would buy those products— Toyotas and little green Datsuns. They already had a foothold here before I realized what a force they would become in our industry and, belatedly, I began to move into the foreign as well as other domestic markets.

So when anyone tries to tell me how smart I am, and praise me as a man of vision, I am able to stay in radio contact with the planet Earth by reminding myself that I am the prophet who lost World War II. I blew it on Volkswagen and the Japanese compact cars.

I can assure you, at such times it helps to have a hero, in my case a father who believed his son, with maybe a rare exception, could do no wrong. I had one of the most devoted fathers of all time.

It takes a special man, secure and humble and unselfish, to work for his son. My dad did it without hesitation, without demands, without conditions. All he wanted was to help, and to let his wife enjoy her granddaughters.

His friends called him Slim or Mac, almost never Willie. He was born on June 5, 1903, the year a Packard reached New York City fifty-two days after leaving San Francisco. It was also the year that Orville and Wilbur Wright flew the first heavier-than-air machine at Kitty Hawk, North Carolina.

Dad was born with a gift for understanding anything mechanical. He was self-taught, and probably was close to being a genius when it came to analyzing what was inside a motor or an engine. He was attracted to airplanes with the same passion he felt for cars. There was a small airstrip in Spur, and he was always down there when the stunt pilots of that era put their planes down. He would literally bombard them with questions.

I believe he forgave me for bailing out on the Edsel. But when I moved my family to San Antonio and reopened the new car dealership, he took a job in Aransas Pass, a small town near Corpus Christi. Mom and Dad visited us one weekend a month. I was just sure that they preferred to live in a smaller town.

I don't want this to come off as sexist, but there is a feminine instinct, one that involves the unseen longings in each of us, that men lack. After we had been settled in San Antonio for a year or so, and the folks had just left from a visit with us, Charline said, casually: "Why don't you ask your father to come up here and go to work with you?"

The suggestion caught me off guard. I mumbled something like, "Why, he would never do that. He likes the small town. He's happy in the Ford garage where he works. He would never move."

Charline said, "Why don't you ask?"

That was Sunday evening. The next morning I called my father at work. I told him how much we enjoyed being with them. I said we had a big operation in San Antonio, and it was a big city, but if he ever thought about leaving Aransas Pass and working in a bigger plant, we would love to have him. And I knew what an asset he would be to our service department.

Within two hours, I had a call from his boss, Walter Boehnke, who had befriended me in many ways over the years. His opening line was, "Red, can I do anything to help you with your problems?"

I was surprised, but I thanked him and asked if he had heard anything in particular. He said, "Mac just came in here and said that you had so many problems, he had to go to San Antonio to help you out. He said I could have whatever time I needed to replace him, but he had to go help his boy."

Mr. Boehnke and I had a nice laugh about that, and I asked him to please keep our conversation just between us, which he did. A few weeks later, my parents moved to San Antonio, and Dad spent the rest of his life working for me.

Every morning he would mosey by the office to say hello and give me a hug. We are a hugging family. Dad was very warm and soft-spoken and really believed that his children could do no wrong. I often said that my father had such confidence in all of us, if one of his kids shot the sheriff at high noon he would have said, "Well, they must have had a good reason."

Charline's perception was right on target. He would never have told me that he wanted to work for me. When I got the chance, I would drop by his work area and visit with him. He liked that, but I liked it even more. To have an opportunity to work with your father for several years is an experience that most people don't get to share.

His memory of detail was spectacular. He could remember people, events, times, dates, and circumstances. He was a slow reader, but he retained everything he read. And he was wonderful at dealing with people, and thrived on fixing their problems. You had a very comfortable feeling in his presence, and when you left you felt better for having been there. No one could fake the concern he showed. That was a plus in our business, where you never hear this from a customer: "Good morning, my car is running perfectly and I want to tell you what a great day it is."

I don't think financial rewards ever figured into my father's definition of success. He couldn't wait to read the technical manuals to see how the new technology worked.

He was fifty-six when he went to work for me. He had been working since he was nine years old, and after a time Charline said, "Why don't you suggest to your dad that he take a month off, instead of two weeks? I think he would love the chance to travel."

I had learned not to question her insights. When I raised the idea, he sort of hesitated and said, "I don't know. You really need me here." But I could see in his eyes that he was receptive. So we worked it out, and then we made the vacation two months, instead of one. That was the schedule for the last five years before he retired.

That subject came up when Charline and I were driving back from a trip to Laredo. She said I should talk to

Dad about his retirement. When I approached him, his response was, "No, I wouldn't have any interest in that at all."

I said, "Think about it. It's not something you have to do right away. But you are pushing sixty-five." When my mother heard about it, she began to consider how much more they could travel, and he sensed her excitement.

So my father retired. We had a nice reception for him, and read a telegram from Henry Ford the Second and a nice letter from President Johnson. Charline and I gave them a going away present, a top-of-the-line motor home and a Texaco credit card. I think it is fair to say they were pleased. Dad was always loyal to the places where he had done busines, and he wouldn't buy gasoline at any station but Texaco.

On a typical trip they would be gone five or six weeks, then come home, stay a week, and take off in another direction. They had become history buffs and traveled all over Alaska and the northwest, meeting old friends and making new ones. Once, I got a call from a friend of mine in Seattle. He said I was wasting my money if I was spending any on public relations. He had just spent ten days in Hawaii, listening to my father, and he had never heard such puffery.

Six years after Dad retired, they were camping out with a group in New Mexico, in the Santa Fe National Forest. As they watched the sunset, Dad took out his New Testament and read aloud from Psalm 24:

"The earth is the Lord's, and the fullness thereof; the world and they that dwell therein. For he hath founded it upon the seas, and established it upon the floods. Who shall ascend into the hill of the Lord? Or who shall stand in his holy place? He that hath clean hands and a pure heart; who hath not lifted up his soul unto vanity, nor sworn deceitfully. He shall receive the blessing from the Lord, and righteousness from the God of his salvation."

Mom and Dad played dominoes until about 10:00 that

night, kissed, and went to sleep. About 2:00 A.M. she heard him groan and utter three words: "Mother, I hurt." She saw him try to sit up, then fall back in his bed. He did not move again. When they called an ambulance, it was already too late.

The date was August 28, 1974. He was seventy-one years old.

Willie Nathan McCombs was a loving and caring man who never pressured his children about what they should do. He was always a booster, a man of compliments, of encouragement. He was extremely proud of what he did, never losing sight of the fact that fixing and repairing machinery was a true talent. In his mind, he probably felt people in management, such as myself, had the lesser role. He was probably right.

CHAPTER 5

IT'S ONLY A GAME

Sometimes I feel sorry for the fans of New York, who have never known the wonders of minor league baseball—not including the New York Mets.

This was once a way of life in America. In 1950 there were only sixteen teams in eleven cities in the majors, two each in New York, Boston, St. Louis, Chicago, and Philadelphia. Everything else was the bushes. At the lower levels, the caliber of ballplaying was not much higher than that of company teams, who played to see who bought the beer.

There was always a railroad track near the ballpark and maybe a bakery, and an organist whose music pumped up the crowd. The players were there to chase a dream, or just for the love of the game. The owners counted their pennies. Whether you made or lost money might depend on the cost of your phone bill.

By 1953, I was doing fine, real fine, selling used cars in Corpus Christi. I had gone into business for myself and opened a second lot. Then I got a phone call from a former classmate of mine at Southwestern, Bob Hamric.

Bob had been an all-around athlete and had signed a contract to play ball in Class A. "Redbird," he said, "I'm doing okay, but I'm not going anywhere. Don't have the skill level. I see where your ballclub down there is going into bankruptcy. Why don't you buy the team and I'll run it for you?"

It started out as one of those conversations you throw away the instant you put the phone down. But Bob came to town and, before I had time to think up any good excuses not to do it, the deal was done. I made Hamric my partner and bought the Corpus Christi Clippers for the princely sum of $10,000 and picked up their debts. I made the rounds of each creditor so the club would not have to take bankruptcy.

We were an independent club, meaning we were not owned by a major league team. We had a working agreement with the Braves, who had moved from Boston to Milwaukee. They held the contracts of half our players. We signed the rest and had our own scouts, who were paid a small fee to seek out talent (that we could afford) in Cuba, Mexico, and South America.

It was Bob's job to assemble a roster. We had taken a team that had lost money and gone bust, and we were having the time of our lives. This is every fan's fantasy—making deals, moving the pieces around.

In the mid-'90s, the NBA made a significant move by adopting a salary cap. But we had a cap in the Big State League forty years ago, even though you couldn't enforce it. The way ours worked, you could pay eighty percent to one player and the balance to all the rest. The club had mostly older players going nowhere and young kids on the way up. We had a pretty decent shortstop making $325 a month, and I sent him a contract that gave him a raise to $340. In that league, an increase of nearly ten percent was significant and, as the new owner, I included a nice letter saying that he deserved it.

When I didn't hear from him, I wrote again, and this time he sent it back, folded and with cutouts, like paper dolls. It read:

Dear Mr. McCombs,
   I don't know you, but you must enjoy a good joke. Enjoy this one.

I called and asked him if we had a problem. He said, "You didn't mention anything about my cash. In addition to the three and a quarter the club has on the books, I get five hundred dollars each month in cash." Welcome to the real world, Red McCombs.

The shortstop, by the way, was no amateur when it came to money. In the off-season, he worked as a plumber.

Thanks to Bob Hamric, the Clippers won the playoffs and the Big State League championship. I was putting people in the stands, paid off our debts, and retired the bank note for the ten grand we had used to buy the team.

Down there in the dungeons of pro baseball, you gained a real healthy respect for a dollar or you didn't last. We had bought the team from the Schepps family, whose dairy supplied milk products to towns all over Texas. It developed that they had not paid the government any withholding taxes. I argued that we didn't owe this money, since it was not a baseball debt.

We exchanged letters and wound up in a hearing with George Trautman, the commissioner of minor league baseball, at the Shamrock Hotel in Houston. Our adversary was George Schepps, a delightful man who spent the better part of his life owning teams in the Texas League and lower.

Hamric, my twenty-six-year-old-partner, and I put on our case. If we owed the local merchants, the bus companies or the cafes where we fed the players, these we had agreed to pay. They were baseball related. But my interpretation did not include the federal government.

Mr. Schepps claimed it was a debt like any other. I'm thinking: *We have been in baseball for a year and here we are in a beef with a man who probably knew Abner Doubleday.*

Trautman listened for an hour, then stopped it. He said, "George, you ought to know better. Taxes are a personal debt. I find in favor of the present owners."

I felt no shame whatsoever about my pleadings. We saved around $3,000. We would have had to sell out the ballpark and have a big run on snow cones to make that kind of money.

George Schepps spent the last decade of his life running and promoting the Texas Baseball Hall of Fame, whose membership included Dizzy Dean, Hank Greenberg, Rogers Hornsby, Carl Hubbell, Joe Morgan, Gaylord Perry, Brooks Robinson, Nolan Ryan, Tris Speaker, and Ted Williams.

Some had a fairly thin connection to the state. Ted Williams managed the Texas Rangers for one miserable season (they lost 100 games in 1972). I'm not sure that Ted cherished that memory in his immortal career. But Schepps believed in a big tent. He was a feisty man right up to his last breath, in 1997, at the age of ninety-four.

I feel privileged to have engaged George in a negotiation, much less to have won it.

After the 1954 season, we attended the winter baseball meetings and I was approached by a man who introduced himself as Robert Creamer with *Sports Illustrated*. I didn't know it then, but Bob was a wonderful writer who later would author an acclaimed biography of Babe Ruth.

He said he had heard that "you guys" have a pretty good operation down in Corpus Christi. I'm thinking: *Here is our chance to attract some priceless recognition.* I laid it on and, sure enough, Creamer wrote a feature story for *Sports*

Illustrated, praising the Clippers as "the best lower minor league operation in baseball."

In our first three years, we continued to thrive on the field. We sent two players to the majors: Don Leppert, a catcher who went on to become a coach with several teams, and Ed Charles, a third baseman and part-time poet. He played on the Miracle Mets of 1969, and gave himself a nickname, The Glider. His teammate, Nolan Ryan, laughs when he thinks about a home run Charles hit in the play-offs, and when Ryan ducked into the dugout he announced, "You never throw a slider to The Glider."

We had a Cuban pitcher, a lefthander named Renee Vega, who claimed to be twenty-six but was probably ten years older, at least. He won thirty-plus games for us, and we were able to sell his contract to a club upstream, but that was as far as he went. We made our money that year by selling off our players to teams in Double-A and Triple-A.

We won our third straight pennant, but attendance was falling off. I could already see the graffiti on the outfield wall. People had fallen in love with the television set. By 1956, those hard slats in a minor league park, the mosquitoes, and the muggy weather were no match for Jackie Gleason and *The Honeymooners* or *I Love Lucy*. I saw the end coming when my best friends, who owed me their loyalty, started to miss a few games.

As objective as I like to think I usually am, I blamed our decline on the local newspaper, the *Corpus Christi Caller-Times.* The beat writer was Roy Terrell, a young, crewcut, good-natured guy. I'd watch the lights of the cars coming into the parking lot, the numbers growing smaller, and I would tell Roy, "If your paper had put a border around that box, we'd have some fans out here."

After Roy had heard all he wanted to hear, he said, "You know, Red, it might be worth your time to look around you. You might find that people have discovered some things more interesting than this raggedy assed baseball team of yours."

He was right, and I apologized. Later, *Sports Illustrated* hired Roy, and his rise was something to see. He eventually became the magazine's editor and then publisher.

Whatever I didn't learn in kindergarten, I learned in the Big State League. Against all the odds, I made over $100,000 and had a helluva good time. But after the 1957 season, I called Hamric and said we ought to get out. Bob thought we ought to buy a club in the Texas League.

I said, "Not me. The difference is, this is slow death. That would be sudden death." Pulling some papers out on my desk, I said, "I'm selling you my stock for ten bucks." I sealed an envelope and dropped it in the mail. I don't know if Bob loved baseball more, or money less, but he stuck it out for three or four more years. It was a financial disaster for him. Later, he had a chance to become a car dealer in Baytown, less than an hour out of Houston, and he called and asked for my help. He bought the dealership and rebuilt his wealth. We would make other deals, including cattle.

This was my romance-with-pro-baseball story, and I wouldn't take anything for it. The elements of running a sports franchise are pretty much the same. Everybody lies to you. They all want to win. They are all competitive. The big difference between running a team in the minors and the majors is the number of zeros on the checks you write.

For example: I am fond of George Steinbrenner. I consider him a good friend. We met through his involvement in the U. S. Olympic Committee, and he has been to San Antonio a number of times. His history with the Yankees is among the looniest in sports. He has fired managers with the frequency of cars crossing the Long Island bridge. No one can name all the managers he has fired or driven away. He just seems to bury them in the window seat, like the little old ladies in *Arsenic and Old Lace*.

But George showed he was more than "The Boss" when his '98 Yankees rewrote the record book and won it all. I think Boss George is one of the best operators in all of the perspiring arts. I would like to do as well.

Sports is no longer a place for your garden-variety millionaire. But the kind of owners I have met are people you would want to spend your time with—risk takers, strong and stubborn.

I once had a problem in the NBA with Jerry Reinsdorf, the owner of the Bulls (and the White Sox). Jerry brought an issue before the league: He wanted to televise more games than our rules allowed. The commissioner opposed him, and the dispute turned into a monstrous lawsuit that is still ongoing. I spoke out against Jerry; to bend the rule might be good for him, but not for the league. Reinsdorf was offended that I would say such a thing. But I said it to his face. I thought he was wrong and still do. It did not affect our friendship.

Wounds are slow to heal and relations among owners are not always blissful. I am not always diplomatic, but I try to be consistent. The more cautious among us will proceed with caution when discussing another owner with someone who might be neutral. For instance, they might start out by saying, "So and so is a jerk, isn't he?"

If the reply is, "No, I think he is okay," then one can add with assurance, "I think so, too." Chances are, however, that if you call one owner a jerk, the others will agree.

I had not met Jerry Jones until he bought the Dallas Cowboys, the most envied franchise in pro football. When the team was finishing 1-and-15 in his first season, I happened to be on a national radio call-in show. The host asked me about Jones. I said, "I know what his plan is and he can execute his plan. He is thinking on a scale where other owners don't go."

Tom Landry had been a friend of mine for as long as I could remember. We worked together in the Fellowship of

Christian Athletes. Jones took a bruising for firing Landry, and yet I thought Tom was wrong in the way he reacted.

Jones had come close to a deal with Bum Bright, who then owned the Cowboys, but it didn't appear to be happening. They had gotten to the trough, backed away, then finally closed the deal. The first thing Jones did was get on a plane and try to find Landry to tell him, face to face, that he was bringing in his own coach.

Anyone who sees that as cold or classless is just not being fair. He faced it head-on, knowing it was a no-win situation. I'm a Landry fan, but I can't fault Jones. As Dear Abby might put it, there is no good way to ask for your ring back.

Jones could not tell Landry and then close the deal. The same applies to the players. Imagine telling one of your stars, "I'm talking to Chicago about trading you. If you hear a rumor, it's true." That deal won't shake. And how much confidence have you inspired in that player? The only way to do it is to make your deal and take your lumps for not telling them in advance.

Yes, you hate for the player or a coach to hear the news on radio or television. All you can do is go to him and try to explain.

Jerry Jones had gotten rich in oil and real estate and was a political power in Arkansas. His old college roomie, Jimmy Johnson, had gained fame as a national championship coach in Miami. In Dallas they were received with hostility, the relationship improving gradually until it consisted mainly of ridicule. Cowboy fans, who had all but called for the public stoning of Landry when the team missed the playoffs, now rallied around him as a martyr.

A big broom swept through the front office. One by one, the last of Landry's Cowboys were retired or released or benched. Having stripped themselves of their veteran leadership, the Cowboys traded Herschel Walker to Minnesota for a bundle of players and draft picks, and laid the groundwork for two Super Bowl champions.

Jones, with his openness and unfailing good humor, didn't turn the fans around, but he did cut his losses. They no longer referred to him as the kind of guy who, if he bought the Vatican, would have fired Mother Teresa.

If there is one absolute, one truth that I have learned about being in sports, it is this: When the team wins, we are all fans. When it loses, we are all experts.

The chance to bring a pro basketball franchise to San Antonio dropped into our laps in 1973. It was a long way from being a slam dunk. The American Basketball Association was struggling, and the Dallas Chapparals were looking for a home.

My friend Angelo Drossos had convinced me to move the team, and we figured out a way to reduce the risk. We would lease the team for $800,000. We had twenty-seven investors, almost enough to qualify us as a public company. I would be the club's first president and would cover twenty-five percent of the first year's losses, with our partners slicing up the rest.

At the last minute, I started to get cold feet. I couldn't find anybody in San Antonio who was excited about basketball except Angelo. He came to my house to talk me into staying on board. In the end, he and Charline kept me from bailing out. She had no interest in the sport whatsoever, but she had heard me talk about this great need to have a major sports franchise in San Antonio. I had been talking about it for years. How could I cut and run when one was finally, literally, on our doorstep?

Angelo was dark-haired, swarthy, fast-talking, very handsome, and personable. I met him when he was operating a bar called The Dragon Lady. He also owned a pair of chili dog parlors, managed some boxers and promoted their fights. A car accident had left him with a shattered arm and a limp, but he wasn't lacking in confidence. When he wanted a regular job, I gave him one, and for five years he was one of my top salesmen and managers.

Angelo agreed to learn the basketball business and operate the club on a day-to-day basis. In the beginning, he didn't draw a salary. He believed the good times were coming, even when I was unsure.

We swallowed hard and closed the deal, knowing we could always cancel the lease and cut our losses. Expansion leagues had been tried before in football and basketball, with an almost comic quality to them. Inevitably, the leagues would begin to shrink, and the challenge was to match the teams that had a place to play with the teams that had an owner.

Our deal was a creative one even by those standards. Somewhere during this time, a phrase became popular with athletes and other artists: In life, it isn't the destination that matters but the journey.

This turned out to be a mighty helpful saying, because we didn't have a clue where all this was going.

To begin with, there was a McCombs family makeover. Neither of us had ever seen much in the way of basketball games—high school, college, or pro. When Charline discovered the Spurs would play forty-five home games, she made it indelibly clear that I should not expect her to see a majority of those. She would pick and choose.

I could and did accept her terms, except for an unforeseen turn of events. After the third game, she was hooked. By the middle of the season, she was suffering from a stomach disorder. She had trouble sleeping. Saw several interns, took all sorts of tests. Once we eliminated the serious stuff, her doctors concluded that her problems were caused by nervous tension—too many close games, too many winning or losing shots at the buzzer.

How do you fix that? Not easy. She didn't want to take tranquilizers. She did take a little medicine, a lot of deep breaths, and occasional glasses of milk. I was concerned about her, but once she knew the source the pains began to fade. Even as intense as I would get, screaming and holler-

ing, I never had that feeling in my stomach of having swallowed a grapefruit wrapped in barbed wire. Well, maybe
once or twice.

She was captured by it almost from day one, and had a
personal relationship with the players and their wives. We
were very much an involved and hands-on couple when it
came to the team.

In November we acquired Swen Nater, the seven-foot
center out of UCLA, from the Virginia Squires for cash and
draft picks. Purely by chance, Swen was going to be the cause
of our first crisis as part-owners of the Spurs. To begin with,
he needed and was looking for a family. Swen had been or-
phaned as a boy in Holland and was reunited with his
mother years later. He married his sweetheart, Maureen, in
San Antonio.

In the summer after his first season, we all vacationed
together in California, drawing the friendship even closer.
Nater was popular with all the fans, but Charline adored
the two of them.

We finished our first season in Hemisfair Arena with a
45-39 record, and Nater was named the ABA's rookie of the
year. In what would turn out to be the most crucial move of
our first ten years, we acquired another rookie from the
Squires in January. His name was George Gervin.

I am not too proud to admit that my knowledge of
pro basketball was zero, and so was Angelo's, but we were
both picking brains, eager to learn. The first time the
Squires came to town, two things really stuck out in my
mind: They had the ugliest uniforms I had ever seen on a
sports team, before or since, brown with orange stripes.
Second, they had some of the most talented players ever
assembled on one team. They had Julius Erving, already
known as Dr. J., Charlie Scott, and the two kids, Nater and
Gervin.

Gervin had dropped out of Eastern Michigan after one
season, making himself available to the ABA draft as "a hard-

ship case," a pretense the pros used to pacify the colleges. I had never seen an athlete suited up to play a game even in high school as skinny as George Gervin. But he moved like a line of poetry. The first time I saw him play, I told Angelo, "We ought to see if we can get this kid on our team."

There was a meltdown in the ABA almost every week. We were at a league meeting in New York and Mike Storen, the commissioner, had announced there would be no more trades, cash or otherwise, with the Virginia Squires. They were trying to sell the franchise, and if the player ranks were depleted any further the only assets would be those ugly uniforms.

Angelo and I had been talking to Earl Foreman, the owner of the Squires, about buying Gervin and had slipped notes back and forth. Storen soon spotted this exchange, grew visibly annoyed, and called a recess. He gave us all a big league ass-chewing, having assumed, correctly, that the notes involved a player transaction and we had been forewarned.

Nevertheless, before the day was over—January 30, 1974—we had agreed on a cash price of $300,000 for Gervin. Knowing that we faced a problem with the commissioner, Drossos began working on the details of the deal. My job was to call the Frost Bank and tell them to wire us $300,000—we had bought another player.

An officer of the bank, Clyde Crews, could not resist asking, "Do you guys know what you're doing?" I assured him we were now experts.

We sent the information in for league approval, and Storen went through the ceiling. "Not only will this transaction not be approved," he roared, "but if Gervin attempts to play for the Spurs, every game will be forfeited."

We laid low for a few days. Angelo made arrangements for Gervin to hide out in a San Antonio motel. The Squires were on the road. After several days of negotiating with Storen, we knew there was no hope of changing his opinion. The Spurs went into federal court and asked for an injunction restraining the league from enforcing this rule.

Judge Adrian Spears enjoined the league and set a quick date for the hearing, clearing the way for us to bring Gervin out of hiding so he could play. Our fans didn't realize, nor did we, that he was going to be the linchpin of our franchise. He went on to play in eleven straight All Star games.

Our fans rallied around us, in effect, for taking the bull by the tail and looking the situation right in the face. The fans love it when you stand up to authority. Still, it was a terrible, cheesy thing to do: the Squires and their fire sale, the Spurs taking advantage of it by defying the commissioner. The judge ruled in our favor and gave us a permanent restraining order. I drove Storen and his lawyers back to the airport, and we were not only civil but friendly.

Still, it was not a good decision and I was in no mood to gloat. You teach your kids to play by the rules. We had violated them with gusto. The results were fine, but the means were less than honorable. I resolved that if the league had any future problems with the Spurs, we would deal with them outside the courtroom.

By the end of the season, you could see the team begin to jell. We had drafted as our first pick George Karl, out of North Carolina. He told me years later that the other guy in our back court, James Silas, was a better player than Gervin.

Karl turned out to be a hard-nosed player who really had his head in the game. He was almost a 100-percent basketball animal, and he battled for playing time that first year. In the ABA, we had a maximum of eight teams, sometimes seven, and we played each other enough times to build up fierce rivalries. George Karl became known as the guy on our club who would take a charge from anybody. He had some classic collisions with George McGinnis, a power forward and a bonecrusher. Karl had a following in San Antonio and made friends for life.

In our second season, the club won fifty-one games. And it soon became clear that Gervin had more talent than most of us would ever see. Which is why the Iceman is in the Hall of Fame, and one of the NBA's all-time Top 50.

The Iceman was not only one of the greatest basketball players who ever lived, he is a great person. Always, without hesitation, he made whatever personal appearances we asked of him. He was a joy to be around, always outgoing, gentle with kids, generous with the media.

After I sold my interest and bought the Denver Nuggets, the Spurs traded George to Chicago. It didn't work for anyone, not George or the Spurs or the Bulls. Fortunately, he saw his jersey retired in San Antonio and today works for the club in community relations, a job I gave him in 1988. He had gone through a long struggle with drug addiction, recognized how destructive it was, and had a terrible time getting that monkey off his back. He did not finally succeed until he went to John Lucas' center in Houston. He got sober and stayed that way and has been a contributor ever since.

I'm not much for climbing on a soap box, but I believe addictions are an illness. Still, not everyone is a victim. Some are just bad apples.

I used to have meetings with the players and staff at the start of every season. I would go through a basic primer of professional sports: "We are in the entertainment business, and this is everyone's job. Let's get down to what is most important to you guys—getting paid. I DON'T PAY YOU. I negotiate your contracts. If I had to pay you, I'd meet one payroll and we'd split the blanket. The fans and the sponsors pay you. Never forget that."

A lot of them would buy into it; some didn't. But I meant every word.

My relationship with the media was always very good. From time to time, I felt I was the target of a cheap shot and I didn't equivocate about saying so. I have called media guys liars right to their faces. They would print something I knew to be untrue, quoting a "source," and I would wonder, why don't I have credibility over that guy?

But I never lost sight of the fact that the media's good will is vital to the health of a sports team. I wanted to do what I could to keep them interested and aware.

All of this is part of what makes sports so important to a city. It is the most ecumenical thing we have. A winning team brings us together. Religion doesn't. Religion divides us. Music doesn't. Some like jazz, others classical, still others country. Business doesn't. If steel prices go up, do Ford and Chrysler exchange high fives?

People in sports should never fear a philosophical discussion. Is this healthy? Is this right? Should we be talking about funding new stadiums, or finding a cure for cancer at M. D. Anderson Hospital? That's the real world. And this is the way things are: Owning a team is not a full-time job, in hours, but it is full-time emotionally. Every place I go, from the car attendant to the chairman of the board, the first words I hear in San Antonio are about the Spurs. You have to understand that, acknowledge that, and respond.

Charline used to frown and shrug her shoulders if someone came up to me and said, "You ought to be playing so-and-so at point guard instead of so-and-so." My response would be, "You know, that's a pretty good idea."

Charline would say, "You don't mean that. Why would you say that? It's dishonest." My answer is, "They don't want to know the reason. They just want someone to agree with them." There isn't time to explain all the nuances of why you do things. Everyone loves it when you agree.

I was making a speech on economic development to a group that was eighty percent female. During the question and answer segment, a woman identified herself and said, "This may not be germane to your speech, Mr. McCombs, but you're the only one who can answer this. I moved here months ago from another state. I find it appalling that so much civic and media attention is put on this silly basketball team. I find it unacceptable. Can you respond to this?"

I said, "Yes, I'm glad you gave me the opportunity. Last night the Spurs played a game before 17,000 people, a sellout. Another 150,000 watched or listened on television and radio. For those hours, they were able to put aside their cares and live or die with their team. In schoolrooms, hospitals and business offices, in homes as neighbors were having coffee, the subject was positive because our team beat the Lakers last night. If that is silly, so be it."

There was a standing ovation, which I did not expect. But the people attending that conference related to the point I was making. Sometimes you need a little candy for the soul.

The feelings I described were familiar to them; they understood. It was personal. All cities have great attributes which are important, and most of us support them: the arts, education, the medical center. Yet there is nothing quite like the impact of a sports team. The people who have trouble seeing that are the ones who have never embraced a team.

To realize how deeply attached the fans become to a team, all an owner has to do is trade away one of the team's most popular players.

After our second season, we lost to Indiana in the first round of the playoffs, four games to two. Bob Bass thought we needed to make a change. He came to Angelo and me and said, "There's a deal out there right now that might not come along again. It would be a chance to strengthen this team."

The New York Nets, he said, had always coveted Swen Nater. (The Nets were not yet in New Jersey.)

My response was, "Who wouldn't? He's a seven-footer, blond, just coming into his own."

Bob said, "A good player, not great, will never be better than he is now. I think you should consider trading him. I think we can get two starters."

In a matter of days, Bob had structured a deal where Swen went to the Nets for Larry Kenon, and we acquired Mike Gale for cash. Weeks later, the second shoe dropped. We sent the Spurs four players who were expendable for Billy Paultz, a wide-track center known as The Whopper.

Kenon and Paultz made the all-star team that year.

The trades were completed with no leaks. No one locally knew about them except Drossos, Bass, and me. The deal was completed late at night, and we had to wait for a conference call with the league office the next morning to confirm the terms. Still, it was a done deal.

That night I went home, sat down to dinner, and realized I had a problem. Charline said, "You can't imagine what happened to me at the beauty shop today. A woman said, 'What do you think about your favorite player being traded?' I said, 'Well, that's wrong. Not only will Swen not be traded, his jersey will be retired here and hang from the rafters.'"

Ironically, the woman who told her this wasn't even a fan. I was choking on every bite of food. Charline and our three girls went to bed, and I stumbled into the library.

I was up early the next morning and called her from the office at 9:00. "Sweetheart," I said, "there is going to be a press conference at ten. I regret to tell you that your friend was right. We've traded Swen to the Nets."

Charline started sobbing on the phone. "If you're going to do things like this," she said, "I think you ought to get out of the business. The players become your friends and you can't treat them that way."

At 3:00 she called me back, unable to contain the excitement in her voice. "Honey, can you come home right away?" she asked. After what had happened, I didn't want to ask her why. I said I would be there in fifteen minutes.

I walked onto the patio, and there was Charline with Swen and Maureen. Charline grabbed me and embraced me and said, "You can't imagine what this sweet guy has done." She turned to Nater, and he was literally too choked up to talk. "Honey," Charline went on, "he's willing to take any kind of pay cut you want to give him. Money isn't that important to him."

All I could do, short of finding a hole to crawl into, was say, "Let's sit down and talk about what happened." I explained that it wasn't a question of money. The deal was done. When you're traded, you have to go where the trail takes you. I felt like a dog, and I left the three of them crying. That was the intensity level Nater had. I don't know of anyone who gets any pleasure out of shipping somebody out, or giving them a pink slip.

Trades rarely make everyone happy. If there is joy on one end, there is usually heartache on the other. After I bought the Spurs a second time, we had a chance to trade Alvin Robertson, who had been an all-star, for Terry Cummings from the Milwaukee Bucks. I had coveted Terry since his senior year at DePaul. Not long after we hired Larry Brown, we completed the trade. I was in the office when Bob Bass was trying to find Alvin to notify him. Bob looked up and said, "I have Alvin on the line."

Larry had just finished talking to him a few hours earlier. He said, "I don't want to do it. You tell him, Red."

So I picked up the phone. Alvin and his wife had been looking at a house they were building in a new, nice section of town. Before I could say much more than hello, Alvin chirped, "Hey, chief, you need to go get Charline and meet us over here. I want to show you our new house."

"Alvin," I said, "I have to tell you this . . . You've been traded to Milwaukee for Terry Cummings." He didn't answer. I heard him say, "Oh, shit," and he apparently just dropped the phone. I was still talking and there was no one on the other end. A few minutes later, his wife came on and said, "Is it true?" I said yes, and the line went dead.

No, breaking the bad news isn't pleasant. It's the one part of the game that never gets easier with practice.

In June of 1976, the four surviving ABA teams—Denver, Indiana, the Nets, and us—merged with the NBA. In 1983 I sold my interest in the Spurs to Angelo and bought the Denver Nuggets.

I was fortunate because Carl Scheer was the general manager of the Nuggets, and I had worked with him in the ABA. He was one of the most creative people in the league. During those years, I had also been impressed with Vince Boryla, who showed he had a nice touch with the players, even with a doomed Salt Lake City team. Vince now lived in Denver and had become wealthy in private business. I convinced him to join us and run the basketball side, with Carl handling the marketing. We had a press conference at McNichols Arena, and I announced that the duties would be split.

Vince drove me to the airport, and on the way I dropped my little bombshell. "I'm so glad to have you aboard," I said. "Now let me tell you what your first assignment is."

Half-joking, Vince let out a stream of expletives. The press conference had only ended a few minutes earlier.

I plunged ahead. "We're under .500, we have only three players anyone would want, Kiki Vandeweghe, Alex English, and Dan Issel, who is near the end of his career. The previous owners dealt away most of their draft choices. I need something to sell this summer."

We had pulled right up to my private plane, and as I was getting out of the car I said, "I want you to trade either Kiki or Alex or both in the next thirty days."

Vince said, "We haven't even talked about this. How are we going to handle trades?"

I said, "You are. You have full authority to make any deal you want. Tell me about it when it's over. I have real strong opinions, and I'd rather trust your judgment than mine."

"What if I make a deal and you don't like it?"

"Then you won't last long," I said, flashing him a big smile. "But I don't expect that to happen."

"Okay, you don't want to know until it's done. But what's so important about thirty days?"

"It can be thirty-five. But I have to have something to sell the fans before the season, and we don't have much more time than that."

Two weeks later he called and said, "On a scale of one to ten, I'm at seven. Do you want to know the team?"

I said no.

"Not even the players we're talking about?"

"No."

Another call: "I'm at eight. Can I tell you now?"

"No."

Vince called again on the twenty-ninth day. "Do you have that plug of tobacco there? You better take a big chew. I just traded your boy Kiki for Calvin Natt, of Portland. What do you think?"

I said, "We need more toughness. He's only six-six but he plays like a seven-footer. How do I evaluate it? Gives us something to talk about, but it's just a deal."

He said, "Well, there's a little more. I got Wayne Cooper, Portland's backup center. We can play him as a backup to Issel or move Dan to power forward. And there's more. We got Fat Lever."

Under my desk, my boots were dancing. "Now that's a happening," I said. "You got three players for Kiki."

"No," he said, "we got three players, and their first and second draft picks." We ended up with four starters. That deal got Jack Ramsay fired as the Portland coach, although I defended Jack to the media and will to this day. He had inventory. He had draft picks. He needed the outside scorer.

The level of pay to the players was very high compared to the average income, and that hasn't changed since 1973. I wanted to be aggressive. I couldn't say that because we were in a small market we couldn't pay the money. What I didn't want was to end up with a player who couldn't play.

Cash trades, which are no longer in vogue, were still significant when I bought the Denver club.

The Utah Jazz were strapped for cash, and I fell in love with the soft, outside jump shot of Danny Schayes, whose dad, Dolph, had been one of the greats in the early postwar years of the NBA. The Nuggets had a center who was nearing the end of his career, a fine defensive player from Stanford, Rich Kelley. I thought a Kelley-for-Schayes swap would really improve our team, and I suggested as much to our coach, Doug Moe, who had been with us in San Antonio in the late '70s.

Doug had his usual delicate response: "You are such a dumb shit. You know we have a soft team. Schayes is soft. We need the toughness Rich Kelley gives us. Forget it."

Well, I didn't forget it. I contacted Frank Layden, the coach and general manager in Utah. He was a large, plump philosopher who defended himself when his weight topped out at 300 pounds: "In India, they would worship this body." (Frank has now lost all that weight and looks terrific.) Layden was known for his one-liners, and every phone call brought a laugh. Talking once about team chemistry, he said, "A good point guard and a good scorer should go hand in hand—but not in the locker room."

Of course, Frank knew a team couldn't win without the right material. "If they gave Michelangelo bad marble," he said, "he couldn't make a great statue."

Layden told me he had no interest at all in trading Danny, a player he had just drafted. I finally offered him Kelley and $100,000 in cash, and he declined. He said he loved the sound of that word—cash—but it was still no deal.

A few weeks later, Frank called me back. He said his cash flow problems were now critical, and he had a proposal for me. "I will trade you Schayes for Rich Kelley and $300,000 in cash," he said, "but I want to tell you as a friend, I don't think you're going to help your club. Even though Danny is younger and will be in the league longer, you need Kelley's toughness. I don't think Doug will let you do this."

It was a hard sell. When I repeated the terms to Moe, he snapped at me: "If you want to throw some money around, give some to me and Big Jane. We can use it. You want to pay me peanuts, and then throw away your dough on that big stiff."

I kept moving the idea along and, finally, Moe agreed. As far as I'm aware, that was the last transaction in the NBA where cash played the major role.

However . . . there was one that might have happened, and if it had, the whole league would have freaked out. It was so big, and so complicated, I have never discussed it with anyone but Charline until now.

I had sold the Nuggets—another story—and reacquired the Spurs in 1988, mainly to keep them from being moved out of town. I paid the market price to Angelo and his group, $47 million. The team had not won more than thirty-five games in any of the past four seasons, and was basically waiting for David Robinson to finish his navy tour and come to the rescue.

Shortly after Dave Checketts was hired as general manager of the New York Knicks, he called and said he wanted to fly to San Antonio and meet with me. I had first met Dave when he did consulting work for a financial company. He left there for management jobs with the Jazz and briefly with the Nuggets, before joining the NBA office. I knew him casually and was impressed with his abilities.

He said he wanted the visit to be totally private, so he checked into a hotel under an assumed name, asked me not to meet him at the airport, and took a taxi to my home. We talked over dinner, a bowl of soup and a sandwich.

The subject he wanted to discuss was trading Patrick Ewing and $10 million for David Robinson.

At the time, I had my own cash shortage, the result of what was referred to in Texas as the financial holocaust. Oil prices had crashed, the real estate market collapsed, banks and savings and loans had gone belly up.

I had plenty of assets, but not much that was liquid. So when Dave made his proposal, I told him I had three observations and it took only a few seconds to rattle them off. Number 1, Ewing had indicated he wanted to renegotiate his contract. Number 2, we had already hitched our star to David and were comfortable with seeing how far he could take us, and Number 3, although $10 million was a fortune, it wouldn't help me in terms of my needs. But $25 million would.

Finally, I needed to know by what authority he could make this deal. He satisfied me that he had the authority to make the offer he had just put on the table, but no more than that.

That was how we left it. I indicated I would do the deal for $25 million in cash; would take my chances on Ewing's contract; and would take the heat in San Antonio that was certain to come after the buildup we had given Robinson.

Checketts flew back to New York and called the next day. He said he had the authority to go higher, but nothing close to twenty-five. I said that was fine, but the amount didn't matter, for twenty-four and a quarter I wouldn't do it. No deal.

By my rationale, the players were probably equal in ability. But I had in David Robinson the kind of player I wanted to build a team around, a perfect fit for San Antonio. His contract had a burdensome provision—every three years he would get the average of the league's top two salaries—but we were counting on him to save the franchise. It's hard to put a price on that.

In retrospect, the $25 million in cash would have untied a few knots in the belly, but as I have always known, tough times never last, tough people do. We worked our way out of it. As for the deal that might have been, this was one the press did not get wind of. Most of them they do. Many are not true. I won't even try to imagine all the consequences of this one. It may sound arrogant, I know, but while $10 million would have been comforting, it was not significant in the world I was dealing in.

What I can say with certainty is that the Spurs are still in San Antonio because of two players, in different decades: George Gervin and David Robinson.

We had to wait two years for David, but his mother and father arrived not long after he left Annapolis. He flew in when he could, spoke to school assemblies, and rode buses all over South Texas, helping to sell our program. He never had that superstar mindset.

I cherish my personal relationships. I can't imagine a meaningful life without them. And status has no bearing on them.

Shaquille O'Neal grew up (and up and up!) in San Antonio and was already a celebrity in high school. When he went to LSU, he stayed in Baton Rouge the summer after his freshman season. His second year, he wanted to come home, and I received a call from Dale Brown, his coach, asking if I could find him a job. I said absolutely. I'd be delighted.

I had met Shaquille and his parents. Shaq and his father, Sergeant Harrison, had come by the dealership, and every eye in the place bugged out. I took them into my office, and when Shaq sat down he seemed to do so in sections—one part, then another. He is a very likeable, very well-mannered man.

His father led the discussion about the job. "What would Shaquille be doing?"

I asked if he had any laboring skills. Were we talking about an administrative job, or parking cars and running errands?

The father said, "Probably the latter."

I said, "That's minimum wage."

His dad looked at me as if I had missed a beat somewhere. He said, "You're not thinking of paying him minimum wage, are you?"

"We never pay anyone other than at the level of the job they are performing," I said. That pretty much ended the meeting. Shaquille never said a word. He was polite and a gentleman. I'm proud of the way he has handled himself as a pro, as a superstar without airs, and I never faulted his father for wanting more money for him.

In my companies, the policy works the other way, too. If a person making $30,000 is performing a job that pays $100,000, he or she gets raised to that salary, even though they might be happy with $40,000.

As a breed, I love the people in sports because, no matter how they isolate themselves and defy time and change, they reflect the outside world. They reflect it in a way that I think benefits society. They seem stranger than other people because they have so little privacy.

I have scored some of my biggest hits and biggest mistakes in the sports category. I made a huge blunder in 1985, when I sold the Nuggets to Sidney Shlenker, a friend from Houston, in a phone conversation that lasted less than twenty minutes.

We liked everything about Denver. We didn't move there, but I had a car dealership and friends, had put together a solid front-office team, loved the weather. But at times, my life has taken turns I can't explain.

Sidney owned ten percent of the Rockets but wanted his own franchise. He called and said he wanted mine. We were winning. He liked our organization.

I told him I wasn't interested in selling.

"Any chance you'd ever be?" he asked.

"Maybe three years or so down the line."

"How much do you think you might sell it for then?"

I tossed out a figure that I thought was outrageous.

"I'll give you that right now," he said.

I thought about it for a heartbeat or two, then said, "I'll take it."

It was a major error on my part. We didn't need the money. There was no pressure to sell. But most of all, I had done it again to Charline. I didn't realize, again, what an emotional blow this would be to her, how attached she had become to the town and to Doug Moe and his wife Janey, and our general manager, Vince Boryla.

She owned two percent and a seat on the board, and she kept them. I couldn't make it up to her. When the genie is out of the bottle, it's gone. I get over hurts, and I put the deal behind me, but it takes Charline longer. I'm not sure she ever did get over this one.

"I was more than a little upset," she told a reporter. "Very unhappy. It came as such a shock. One day we were one big happy family in Denver. The next day Red called to say he had sold the team."

If the reader will permit me, this is my chance for some serious groveling. I've always said that I've never owned anything. I'm a salesman. I've only signed one lifetime contract, and that was with Charline. So far, I'm pleased to say, she hasn't tried to renegotiate it.

CHAPTER 6

COACHES I HAVE KNOWN

In terms of job security, coaching a professional basketball team has been compared to being a migrant fruit picker. I admire them because most coaches are a little crazy and they don't try to deny it.

Of course, there is no science to hiring a coach—or firing one. As owners, and fans, we all want the same mythical figure: a genius who can inspire the players, outwit his rivals, and charm the media. In the euphoria of success, he remains modest and calm and stable.

If he fails, we wish him well in his next endeavor. It isn't fair, but you reach a point of no return. The losses are piling up. The players have tuned him out. The boos of the fans build in volume, causing the arena to vibrate, like elephants shaking a bridge into collapse by walking across in cadence. Sometimes a change is the only option you have.

We started out in San Antonio with Tom Nissalke, who had been with the franchise in Dallas. The ABA was still struggling, and in our desire to spread the risk we may have gone a little overboard. We led the league in partners, with twenty-seven.

Nissalke was smart and eager, with the eye of a teacher. When he was an assistant coach at Milwaukee, the writer Roger Kahn followed the team for a few weeks for a magazine story. Kahn was then working on his book *The Boys of Summer,* about the Brooklyn Dodgers of the 1950s.

It says something about Nissalke, and his curiosity, that Kahn would meet with him after the games for a drink. "He'd want to talk about basketball," said Tom, "and I'd want to hear those baseball stories and talk about writing.

"He told me how he got the idea for the book. He was doing a story on Billy Cox and he found him tending bar somewhere. When Roger walked in, the first thing Cox did was turn to his customers and yell, 'This guy is a writer. He'll tell you. Who was the best third baseman in the game? Tell 'em, tell 'em!' And Kahn said Cox was, and he meant it. He got to wondering what had happened to the other players. They all had one thing in common. They all wanted to hold on to their finest hour . . .

"I read a newspaper article later; a writer had gone into the Yankee locker room and asked a bunch of the players what they would have been if they hadn't gone into baseball. One said a doctor. Another said he probably would have been a lawyer. Or a movie star. But Mickey Mantle said, 'Truck driver,' and Whitey Ford said, 'Bartender.' They were the realistic ones."

I liked and respected Tom. But we needed to create fans, and his style was structured, sound, short on excitement. I didn't see us playing the up-tempo game other teams were playing. I knew very little about basketball, but in the front office we had Bob Bass, who knew the game at every level and loved to run and gun. In early December of 1974, Bass replaced Nissalke. The team finished with 51 wins and second place in the western division.

Bob did a great job from day one, as he did in all the different roles I asked him to undertake during my time with the Spurs. He was, in the best sense of the phrase, the ultimate organization man—loyal, unselfish, always available.

Then, in 1976, the Spurs were accepted into the NBA along with Denver, Indiana, and the New York Nets. It was the right time to retool, and Bob stepped aside. Doug Moe was the new coach, with Bass showing his class by serving as Doug's assistant.

Doug had been a favorite of mine as a player. He was a happy-go-lucky type who loved the wide-open game and believed that it was acceptable for coaches to laugh and have fun. In San Antonio, and later Denver, his teams became known for almost blowing out the scoreboard lights.

Angelo Drossos had fired Cotton Fitzsimmons and replaced him with Bob Weiss, a good man and a studious but uninspiring coach.

It was at this point that I reenlisted as the majority owner of the Spurs. In this resurrection, I hired three coaches who rank high on my list of risks taken, gambles won or lost. Each in his own way was a special talent, with little common ground in style or personality. Whatever fate held for them in San Antonio, we shared vivid times, and I enjoy their friendships to this day.

Larry Brown has a fine face, a slight build, and a big brain. He played and got his coaching start under Dean Smith at North Carolina. Larry is driven and demanding, of himself as much as his players. He has won wherever he has gone, and that is a high compliment because few coaches have moved around as much as Larry Brown. Guys who sell stock in phony uranium mines don't move around as much.

At the time I called him, in 1988, he had already coached six NBA and college teams. He had just won the NCAA championship at Kansas, then caused something of a storm. He accepted the UCLA job and then, at the press conference where he was to be introduced, stunned his audience by announcing that he had changed his mind.

What propels Larry isn't clear, but he moves fast and in an orbit all his own.

When he rejected UCLA, the team that had dominated college basketball under John Wooden, I allowed my imagination to take a leap. I had to think hard about Larry Brown's nervous feet, but the Spurs were at a crossroads—as we frequently were. We had the lowest attendance in the league, the lowest ticket prices, the lowest everything. Hiring Larry would cure our credibility problems. We had signed David Robinson, and now had to wait until he finished his service in the navy. I knew we were not going to win until David had time to develop.

To negotiate with Larry Brown, it was first necessary to find him. In a few days I did, and we had a warm and easy conversation on the phone. I congratulated him on winning the Final Four, and then I got to the point.

"Larry, my plane is gassed and ready to go. I need to meet with you today."

"What about, Red?"

"I need your help. We need you to take over this team."

"Oh, Red. I kind of embarrassed myself. I'm staying at Kansas." He was soft-spoken, almost diffident.

I kept pressuring him. I asked him if I could see him in two and a half hours. My Lear jet could fly to Manhattan in two.

Finally, he agreed to meet with me the next morning. I took Bob Bass along, and all the way there he kept saying, "You'll never get this done."

It really didn't seem logical that Larry would walk away from UCLA and a job that was pure gold, go back to Kansas, then walk away again to come to San Antonio. But this trip wasn't about logic. I had decided that we had to have him, his ability, his record, his name. I really believed that he was our best chance of keeping the Spurs in town, and perhaps our last chance to have big league sports for a number of years.

I already had $47 million on the line, and that investment had stretched me big-time. I wanted Larry Brown as my coach, and I wanted him that day.

Just the three of us met that morning. I talked for a solid hour, barely taking a breath. In the end, he asked me one question: "Who will make the basketball decisions?"

I said, "You and Bob will have to submit the big ones to me. If you both agree, it's damned unlikely I wouldn't do it. If you want something and Bob doesn't, submit it anyway. If Bob wants it and you don't, we won't do it."

We had a deal. Money and terms never came up in our talk with Larry, and I was in no mood to drag it out with Joe Glass, his agent. Joe asked for a base salary of $400,000 and incentives worth about $275,000.

I got tired of hearing the agent recite his list, and so I asked him to come up, quickly, with a total. "It's about $675,000," he said.

"Then I'll just make it $700,000, total, guaranteed."

We had a press conference the next morning. My first thought was, how can we get Larry in front of the most people? And it came to me—I called the manager of the largest shopping center in town. We would "Brown Bag" it at lunchtime. I had sack lunches fixed for me, Larry, Bob and Charline, and the manager invited the shoppers to do the same. We filled the mall with thousands of people, and Larry stayed for three hours, signing autographs and chatting with the fans.

We won only twenty-one games in Larry's first season, when Willie Anderson, from Georgia, made the all-rookie team and led the Spurs in scoring. But our marketing, and sales of tickets and suites, went through the roof. I knew we were on our way.

In 1990 and 1991, Larry coached the team to 56 and 55 victories and won the Midwest. David Robinson had shed his sailor suit, joined the team, and led us in nearly every category. In the only discordant notes, we lost in the playoffs to Portland in the semifinals and to Golden State in the first round.

Jack Ramsay, the longtime NBA coach, once said that Magic Johnson "has a 24-second clock in his head," which sounds mighty uncomfortable even for an all-time great. The remark was a tribute to Magic's ability to milk the clock and get off a shot.

Larry Brown carried a calendar in his head, and it had a timing device of its own. The lingering question about Larry's tenure with the Spurs was whether he quit or was fired. I'll let the reader decide.

As anyone who knew him was aware, no one took defeat any harder. Losses left Larry depressed. He reacted to them like a death in the family. In January of his fourth season, the team had not been playing well. We lost three out of four on the road to Golden State, Chicago and Boston, games Larry felt we should have won. We were 21-17 when we came home to meet the Clippers.

Before the game, Larry took me aside and said, "Red, you need to get another coach. These guys are not going to respond to me. There is more talent here than I'm getting out of them."

I could see how downcast he was, but I found his words upsetting. There are two kinds of momentum in sports. One carries you along on wings of eagles. The other drops you like a rock down a drainpipe. Players take their cue from the coach.

I said, "That's dangerous, Larry. You need to quit talking that way."

"I'm either going to quit, or you need to fire me."

"Okay, I'll fire you, but first you need to go back to your room and think about it." I quickly found Gregg Popovich, his assistant coach, and told him what had happened. I said, "Go get him and pull him back together."

All Gregg could say was, "Oh, shit!"

When Gregg called, he said he thought Larry would be okay. He called again after practice and said everything was fine.

I had a business meeting downtown the next day. A waiter slipped me a note: "Call Joe Glass immediately." Larry's agent. Not a good sign.

"Red, we need to talk about this," he said.

It was clear that Larry had worked himself into a torment. He wanted out. My attitude was basic: You have not been fired when an owner is trying to talk you into staying. Larry Brown could have coached for me as long as he wanted.

So I asked Bob Bass to come back for the fourth time and coach the team the rest of the year. Rod Strickland held out for the first six weeks. David tore a ligament in his thumb and missed the final fourteen games. We finished with a 47-35 record, second in the Midwest, swept by Phoenix in the first round of the playoffs.

A day or two after the wire services spread the news of Larry Brown leaving, I received a phone call from a man I had never met. He was calling from Las Vegas. Jerry Tarkanian said, straight out, "Red, I see Larry has left and I want that job."

I was impressed with his directness, and how easy it was to talk to him.

"Have you got anybody in mind to replace Larry?" he asked.

"No. I don't plan to replace him until the off season."

I'm sure some people would be turned off by this kind of call, these blunt questions from someone they had never met. Not me. I knew Tarkanian's background, his unbroken string of successes, his running battles with the NCAA investigators.

I told him, truthfully, that it was very unlikely that I would hire a college coach. He said, "Would you mind if I called from time to time?" I said not at all. We became telephone pals.

He would call two or three times a week, and I was growing more and more impressed. I mentioned this to Bob Bass, who put his head in his hands and said, "Oh, no, Red. No matter how great a coach he is, we need to stay with the pros."

The Spurs were flying to Los Angeles to face the Lakers, and Jerry and I made arrangements to meet for the first time. We had been talking on the phone for about a month.

I had to make the arrangements, and the CIA could not have been more discreet. I had someone else leave the tickets, so the media wouldn't get curious. I planned to take my seat at the last minute and we would be sitting in different sections. We would meet in the morning at a place I picked, fifteen miles from the hotel, not known as a sports hangout.

Charline and my daughter Lynda rode out with me on the team bus to the Forum, as we always liked to do. While the players were getting dressed, I went to the floor to kill time, visiting with the broadcasters and people who worked for the Lakers. Charline and Lynda dropped by the Forum Club.

There were fewer than a hundred and fifty people in the building, just the early birds. The doors were not even open yet to the general public. The Spurs had left the locker room and were going through their shoot-around. I took a seat in the fourth row and, like locusts, here came a swarm of reporters from every direction. As they descended on me, I thought, *Good Lord, what's happened?*

They peppered me with questions: "Have you already hired Tarkanian? What exactly is the deal?"

I looked at them and was pleased that I could say quite honestly, "I have not only NOT hired Jerry Tarkanian, I have never met him. Never seen him."

No one asked if we had talked. They were shaking their heads, wondering where such rumors come from, how they get started.

I learned later what had happened. As any basketball fan knows, Tarkanian has a very recognizable profile. Charline and Lynda were in the Forum Club when he walked in. They knew of our phone calls, and I had never told them I was keeping our talks a secret. They walked over, introduced themselves, and joined him for a drink.

Charline and Lynda were tickled when they rejoined me just before the tipoff. "You'll never guess who we just met," they said. Oh, yes, I could.

After the game (we won it, 102-94), I was walking to the visitor's dressing room, and passed by the door to the Lakers' quarters. There was Tarkanian, with a crowd of people around him. I couldn't avoid him. I held out my hand and said, "Coach, I'm Red McCombs of the San Antonio Spurs."

He said, "Oh, so nice to meet you."

I went inside our locker room, having effectively killed the story—for the time being.

I did not offer Jerry the job at breakfast. But in the cab going back to our hotel, I told Bob Bass, "I'm going to hire him."

Bob said, "No, Red, please. At least wait until the season is over before you decide."

As soon as the season ended, all I kept hearing was, "Who are you going to hire? Are you interested in so-and-so?" I heard that Chuck Daley wanted the job, but I never learned if he really had any interest. I never asked him. I wanted Tark and the turbulence he brought with him.

I slipped him into town without a news leak and even hid him in a room next to the press conference without his being seen. My excitement led me into one of my more embarrassing boo-boos.

The reporters gasped when I brought him in, setting up

his appearance with the words, "I want to introduce you to the new coach of the San Antonio Spurs, Jerry Tarkington." I said it twice.

Still, in spite of that slip of the lip, I was happy. I knew he was a winner, and he would bring new life to the team and even the city.

Let me tell you about Tarkanian. He won a national championship at Nevada-Las Vegas, and just missed another. He also made the Running Rebels the most hunted team in the history of college basketball, unfairly I thought. And the courts later agreed. He engaged in an endless series of battles with the NCAA, where he had a rap sheet longer than Manute Bol's arms. Sworn to bring him to justice, all the NCAA's agents really did was make him take his act out of town. In the end they were found guilty of conspiracy and paid millions to settle the lawsuit.

In a town that worships a winner, Tarkanian won at an 81 percent clip, playing in a field house paid for by state taxes on slot machines. This is a guy who made the desert bloom.

Of course, the transition from college to pro is not a sure thing. The critics asked how he would fare in a league where no one cares what anybody did more than twenty-four seconds ago. Would he lose whatever edge he had in Las Vegas, where the Rebels were not exactly a shining example to the youth of America?

After they won the title in 1990, a reserve forward named Moses Scurry was asked how they did it. "We a well-in-shape team," he replied.

But I was confident that the colorful variety of players he recruited in Las Vegas would benefit Jerry, when it came to dealing with the pro temperament.

When Anthony Avent—now there's a name out of Wuthering Heights—was asked to compare one year's Las Vegas lineup to the next, he said: "Different team, different sha-boom."

I believe this was Jerry's undoing in the NBA. He could not transfer the sha-boom. Even the good teams get blown out a dozen times a year, a reality the Shark found hard to accept. He had been a college coach for thirty-two years and, for all the running and gunning, his teams played terrific defense.

The mix may have been wrong in San Antonio, and his critics would cut him no slack. Abe Lemons, the former University of Texas coach, a folksy humorist and a man I respect, liked Jerry and defended him. "It was easy to go after Tarkanian," he said, referring to the NCAA and his other critics. "He LOOKS guilty. He looks like he just got off a boat with an armload of rugs."

With his bullet-shaped head and dark, hooded, mournful eyes, Tarkanian was a different presence in the pros. Ten or twenty years ago, he might have slam-dunked the league. But he did the one thing he could ill afford to do. He did not trust his own instincts. Just as Jerry got my attention by using the phone, he loved to get opinions from people all over the league. It didn't occur to him that they might have their own agenda. His sources told him he didn't have a point guard, this guy is overrated, that one lacks grit.

All I asked him to do was use his own judgment and do the things that worked for him before. The floor was the same size. So was the basket.

I have no doubt that he could have been a great coach in the NBA, but he let other people poison his mind. So his pro career lasted twenty games, eleven of them losses, and you could see the pain on Tark's face—the fear the season would never end. This is not an uncommon feeling among NBA coaches, but none of the others carried the burden of Tarkanian's success in the college game.

The day he got fired, December 18, 1992, the week before Christmas, I hadn't even planned to visit with him. I had a speech to make for the United Way. Meanwhile, Bob Bass and Gary Woods were huddling in the Spurs' office, working on the budget. I stopped by and was going over a few points, when Tarkanian appeared. We had lost a game in Houston the previous night, in the last few seconds. In the dressing room, Tark thought he was having a heart attack, but it turned out he was simply dehydrated. They held the plane for him.

He heard I was in the office talking to Bob and Gary. He was concerned about his symptoms and what was causing them, namely, the team.

"I've got to talk to you," he said.

"I can't," I told him, "I have a speech to make to the United Way and I'm just leaving."

"I've got to talk to you, NOW," he repeated.

We didn't plow any new ground, but Tark got very emotional about the lack of talent. He told me that with the players he had, the team could not play .500 ball.

This attitude startled me. I had expected a period of adjustment. The slow start had not rattled me. I tried to turn Jerry's attention to the team's history. I had been in the league, off and on, since the mid-'70s. I told him this team would not only play .500 ball, it would play for the Western Conference title.

He shook his head. "You misled me," he said, "on the ability of these players." While Tark was venting, I decided he was through. I said, "Coach, excuse me a minute. I've been here longer than I thought. I've got to make a call. You need a Coke or anything?"

I ducked into Bass' office and said, "Bob, see if you can get John Lucas on the phone. [He had founded a drug rehab center in Houston, and was back there after coaching a team in the Continental League.] Number 1, ask him if he wants to coach the Spurs. Number 2, if the answer is yes, ask him to do an evaluation of our roster . . . just two sentences on each player. Then tell him I may be calling and to stand by the phone."

I picked up a Coke and went back in to see Coach

Tarkanian. I needed to buy a little time while Bass tried to locate Lucas. So I said, "Coach, let's go over this again." And Jerry jumped on my invitation, unloading all over again the flaws and failings of our players.

In a few minutes, I excused myself to go to the restroom. Bass was waiting for me, nervously. Luke was standing by the phone. The answers were yes and yes, and here's his evaluation.

I was so hyper I couldn't read Bob's handwriting, but the analysis was basically very positive. He thought the team had the potential to win 70 percent of its remaining games.

I took a deep breath and said, "Okay, Bob, call Luke and tell him here's what his contract is going to be and it's not negotiable. If he wants to do it, tell him to book a seat on the Southwest Airlines' flight at four. If he can't make that one, get the flight at five. You can pick him up."

Bass said, "Red, I like Luke, but I'm asking you not to do this."

I asked him why.

"Too much trauma. This team can't take all this."

"But you agree Luke is qualified to coach in the NBA. I've been telling you for five years I was going to find a place in this organization for him. This is it. You call John and see if we have a deal."

I had to go back to Tarkanian and do some more double-talk. I was not comfortable with this act, but I was sure we had reached a point of critical mass. Tark was still ranting about how bad the team was. I excused myself again.

By now, Bob Bass was trembling, not because of the risk, but because of the mental exertion of the past half hour. He said, "He's coming. Luke will be on the five o'-clock plane."

"Get with our PR people," I said, "and set up a press conference. Don't say who the coach is. The press conference is only to say that Jerry Tarkanian has been fired."

I went back to Jerry. "Coach," I said, "you were my friend when you walked in this door and I want you to be my friend when you walk out. But as of this moment, you are no longer the coach of the Spurs. The reason is, your expectation level is so low compared to mine, they are never going to mesh."

His jaw dropped. "I didn't mean to get you so upset," he said.

In fact, I was now completely calm. "I'm not upset," I said, "but it's over."

"Well, let's wait a minute," said Tark. "Antoine Carr will be well in a day or two. I can—"

"It's over," I said. "You're not coaching tonight."

"It's four o'clock," he said, his forehead wrinkling, "and I'm not coaching tonight? Who is going to coach?"

"Rex Hughes," I said, naming one of his assistants.

Jerry left without another word, and an hour or so later I announced that he was out. Bob Neal of ESPN was in town, and our press conference was covered nationally. I wanted to get two bangs for my buck. But I also was moving with caution. Lucas had just heard the news on the phone. I wasn't counting my chickens until he was on the ground in San Antonio and we were hugging each other.

The arrival and exit of Larry Brown had been a big story. Tarkanian had been a brief and convoluted one. But Lucas would be the most interesting of all, and the most dramatic.

I hurried over to the locker room to inform the assistant coaches. They were stunned. They had no idea and, of course, there was no way they could have known. I hadn't intended to fire Jerry Tarkanian.

Rex Hughes would take over the team for the night. Then I went in and told the players the events of the day. It was hard to read them. I said, "When you go out to warm up, I don't want you talking to any reporters. You can talk to them tomorrow. We have a game tonight." I walked out, the room eerily silent behind me.

In between parting ways with Tarkanian and the start of the press conference, I squeezed in a call to Charline. I said, "Honey, you better turn on the news. There's a press conference at five."

She said, "I don't have to watch the news. You fired him, didn't you?"

"Before I answer, tell me why you would be so perceptive."

"I could see it coming," she said, "from the way he was talking."

"What about what I was saying?"

"That's just it. You weren't saying anything."

I was in for another surprise. Charline asked me when I was going to announce the new coach. I told her after the game. "Well, is Luke here?" she asked.

I nearly dropped the phone. "How the hell did you know that?" I asked. She was doing an Agatha Christie number on me.

"It wasn't hard," she said. "You've always wanted to give Luke a chance to coach. The new man had to be available and he had to be someone you had no doubts about. And if he was much more than an hour away by air, he couldn't get here."

John Lucas had played for the Spurs, among other teams. We had watched him hit bottom and bounce back from the wreckage of drug addiction. Now he was helping others. Charline loved him. We all did. I knew at least in part how the media was going to play it: Red McCombs was giving an ex-junkie a chance to coach in the NBA. It would have been a major story, no matter who the characters were.

Still, even as the clock was racing, and my mind with it, I felt a strong sympathy for Tarkanian, the Shark. He was a great guy and a great coach, but in San Antonio he had been a fish out of water.

At the press conference, I spoke highly of him and let it go at that. I knew this was not a sub-.500 team. I conferred one more time with Bass. He said, "I pick up Luke, he gets in at six, just in time to talk to the players and coach the game tonight."

"He ain't coaching tonight," I said.

"But," Bob objected, "I told him he was."

"Just tell him he ain't. He has to be incognito. But as soon as the game is over, I want him in the dressing room before the players shower. Put him in with the engineer, up in the Jumbotron."

Bass didn't see the need for all the deception. "Luke comes to half our games," he pointed out.

I said, "Yeah, but this is different. When I give the sign, you bring in Luke." I had drawn up a one-page contract. "When he steps off the plane, you get Luke to sign it."

In the arena, the buzz was everywhere. The crowd had heard the news in a stream of bits and pieces. It was like fireworks going off.

Bob was seated ten rows below me, to my right, and I had told him to bring me the signed contract as soon as he had concealed Lucas. As the game got under way, he hadn't brought it. I made eye contact with him before the half.

Bass came to my aisle and whispered, "Luke hasn't signed it. No problem, but he has to tell his agent."

I said, "I don't care if he tells his agent . . . if he can find him. But if I don't have a signed contract in my hand, he's a spectator. This has been too big a day to leave that big a loose end."

A few minutes later, Bass handed me an envelope with three copies of the contract inside, all signed.

You never know how teams will react to disruption and confusion. But our guys were terrific, blowing out Dallas, 122-101. After the game, we followed our usual custom and went into the locker room. I'm already inside when the players start filing in, high fiving each other because they won.

I congratulated Rex—he is undefeated as a head coach—and I worked the room, hoping that Bass had Lucas waiting outside. I opened the door a crack, and there they were. I said, "Just a second."

I raised my voice: "Listen up. Congratulations, guys. Now I want you to meet the new coach of the Spurs." You could hear a canary feather drop. I let it stay that way for maybe fifteen seconds, then I hit the door and Lucas walked in.

"What, isn't there any excitement for the new coach?" I asked, and then the place exploded.

I will never forget what Lucas said to the players: "Guys, you are the most out-of-shape team I have ever seen in professional basketball. And that goes for you, Mr. Robinson. I know we have a game to play, but we start two-a-day practices tomorrow. We're not going to take a month to get in shape. I'll see you tomorrow."

Then John walked out to face the press conference. The sad note was seeing Rex Hughes standing there. I hated that. His moment of fame had lasted for just about the fifteen minutes Andy Warhol had said everyone would have. Otherwise, no one could have written a better script. The reporters were not expecting a new coach to be announced.

I sat down at the microphone and said, simply, "I want you to meet the new coach of the Spurs." Lucas slid into the seat beside me and fielded the questions.

"I'm going to find out," he said, "if they have the will to win. Among those out there, who won't let you lose?"

There were two fallouts I had not expected from this decision. Neither of them was a part of my thought process, even though they have touched a big part of my life.

The first was the reaction from the black community, from CEOs to the working man, who said: "Hey, you gave a guy a chance who already had two strikes against him."

The other was from people who said, "You have shown that a person can have an addiction, overcome it, and contribute at the level of upper management." I had so many responses along that line, it was humbling. I received letters from people who said, "I have an addiction. Thank God, I'm sober, but I have been black-balled from going up the ladder. You gave a chance to a guy who not only was addicted, but the whole country knew it."

The reaction was both beautiful and meaningful. Regardless of how many games John Lucas won for us, the results were overshadowed by the message sent to tens of thousands of people who shared his experiences. I didn't hire him out of any sense of nobility. But the example it set was by far the most important facet of this decision.

Having said this, I ought to admit that it is part of my nature to lean toward giving an edge to the underdog. Having been addicted to alcohol, which is so hard for people to understand, I know what a blessing it is once you get sober. You are so grateful for your second life. You realize that if you had stayed on the side of addiction, you were dead. So you rejoice in the new life.

Sometimes, in spite of yourself, you look like a genius or a hero. You fall into a mud hole and come out with a bottle of Arpége under each arm.

I had found myself in urgent need of a coach who could hold together the fragile psyches of a team in near disarray. The previous coach had shown little or no confidence in them. Lucas had a huge advantage. They knew him. He had been in the league. He had helped some of them with their personal problems.

So the team responded by winning twenty-four of their next twenty-eight games under Lucas, a surge so unlikely in the NBA that you would compare it to catching lightning in a thimble. We finished with forty wins in our last sixty-six games, close to the seventy percent goal I had envisioned. It was a goal that did not intimidate Luke.

He had played for the Spurs in '83 and '84, after breaking into the league with the Houston Rockets in 1976. He was the first pick in the NBA draft that year as a point guard out of Maryland. And it was there, in Houston, where his story almost ended, ten years later. Lucas woke up from a night he could not remember, wandering through the downtown streets, his shoes missing, his clothing soiled, unable to find his car.

He missed practice that morning, failed a drug test later that day, and sat through a game against Portland in a suit and tie. This was in March of 1986, and his life seemed irreversible. The tragedy was this: Nothing in his life, not his family, his career, his teammates, his reputation, not even money, that he held so dear would rank ahead of the moment of pleasure he enjoyed from drugs.

If a bright, attractive, talented, savvy fellow like John Lucas couldn't figure it out, who could? He was no reject, no dropout, but the product of a stable home, the son of two educators, good enough at tennis to play the game for a living. There was nothing to dislike about the fellow who had been quickly dubbed "Cool Hand Luke."

Whatever else he may have accomplished, he has to be given a ton of credit for rescuing his life, and for helping so many others. He spent two seasons taking the Spurs to the playoffs, winning fifty-five games with a team that Tarkanian labeled a loser.

When I sold the team, one of the sad side effects was the inability of Lucas and the new owners to find a comfort level. He resigned and moved on to Philadelphia, but he made the mistake of doubling as coach and general manager, a task I regard as unworkable. A handful can do both, but most can't.

If Luke had stayed with the Spurs, I believe we would have broken through that veil with Dennis Rodman—and I don't mean the wedding gown and veil he once wore to a book signing. Dennis may never overcome his adolescent traits, but no one ever gave a bigger effort—when he was in the mood.

When we tried to trade for Rodman with Chuck Daley, the Detroit coach said, "The big issue is how the other eleven guys in the locker room react. He is going to test you. It worked for him for two rings (and later a third with the Bulls). But when we (the Pistons) started to slip, things started to fall apart. The key is not the media and not the fans. It's the other eleven guys."

They all knew this. Luke had discussed it with the team. But after Dennis arrived in San Antonio, in my opinion the players were intimidated by him and his behavior. The hair colors, the smirking on the bench, taking off his shoes, holding up signs. All of this was magnified in the playoffs, when the pressure was on.

But the reaction to Rodman was never neutral—not in San Antonio, not anywhere. Since I am so identified with the Spurs, the conversation in those months would nearly always turn to him. People would ask me, "Why do they put up with a guy like Rodman?" I found it interesting that of the people who went to the arena and saw him play, 95 percent were in his corner. Of the people who just read about him, 95 percent were always down on him.

John Lucas didn't last in Philly, but he has been through the fire. No setback is so large that it can bring him down. He went back to Houston, where he runs a tennis club and works with a drug treatment center that is a model for others across the country. I expect to see him back in coaching.

His was a long slide into drug and alcohol addiction, and his recovery may have been among the most public in all of sports. He went from fame and glory to the minor league pits, then suddenly into a high-profile, high-wire coaching job in the NBA. If you needed a title for his career, you might try "Death and Resurrection."

"I like who I am," he once told me, with no self-consciousness. "I don't like some things I did. I made some wrong choices. I had to accept a lot of pain that night in March of 1986, sitting on the bench and knowing I had told two of the biggest lies of my life. But I was afraid to ask for help. Bill Fitch saved my life."

The lie was his insistence, up to the moment the test results were returned, that he was clean. Fitch, then the coach in Houston, forced him to seek help by kicking him off the team and out of the game he loved. "That year the Rockets went to the finals," Luke recalls. "In the '90s, they won two championships. But March 14, 1986, was my championship because I became free from this burden. It was the day I became sober."

Along the way, petty minds did their best to humiliate him. After his first suspension, he was lined up for a free throw when a heckler yelled out from the stands, "Don't snort the foul line, Lucas."

In Milwaukee, the public address announcer wouldn't call his name out after a basket. In another town, he walked onto the court, unaware that a fan who patted him on the back had slapped an adhesive sign to his jersey that said: "Things Go Better with Coke."

A leather lung in Houston stayed on him night after night, calling him a druggie. They saw each other again at a meeting of Alcoholics Anonymous. Now they are friends.

He understands the inner child as few of us ever get a chance to do. "As a young kid," says Lucas, "looking back, I am Jennifer Capriatti. I am very much Monica Seles. We never grow up. We are pushed and pampered as young athletes and move into an adult world overnight, as Andre Agassi talks about it. You get into this competitive mold, and you don't know when to shut if off. I got addicted because I was always competing. I can buy a more expensive suit than you. I can buy a bigger car, have a bigger high.

"My life isn't about winning anymore. It's about acceptance. I forgot about trying to get people to fit into my box. I sat in on an AA meeting with a group of gays and lesbians. I said to myself, ten years ago, I couldn't have been in this room. Today it doesn't matter. I accept people not for what they are, but who. I hope they can accept me the same way."

Under the circumstances, it doesn't seem too much to ask. Which may explain why I don't always judge a coach by his wins and losses. That's one way, but not the only way.

Red McCombs, 1927, Spur, Texas.

Red McCombs with mother and father, W.N. & Gladys McCombs, and sister.

April 5, 1929—Red McCombs' father, W.N. McCombs (middle), at Ford garage in Spur, Texas.

Red at age fifteen, Percy Place Residence, Corpus Christi, Texas.

High school graduation photo, age sixteen.

Red and Charline, wedding photo, November 9, 1950.

Red McCombs and Dennis Walker, first franchise Edsel, Corpus Christi, July 1957.

New T-Bird showing, 1960 (Charline McCombs in middle).
—Zintgraff Collection

Austin Hemphill and Red McCombs announcing dealership name change to Hemphill-McCombs Ford, 1960.
—Zintgraff Collection

Ernest Wood gets $1,000 first prize in Hemphill-McCombs slogan contest, 1961.
—Zintgraff Collection

McCombs displaying Ford Motor Company Award, 1972.
—Zintgraff Collection

McCombs and Austin Hemphill become partners, Hemphill-McCombs location at 1025 San Pedro, San Antonio, 1964.
—Zintgraff Collection

L-R Arjay Miller, president Ford Motor Company, McCombs, Edsel Ford, 1964.

Red handing T-Bird keys to disc jockey Ricci Ware during promotion, circa 1968.

—Zintgraff Collection

Filming a McCombs commercial, 1964.

—Zintgraff Collection

Red and Charline dining at French ambassador's dinner, HemisFair, San Antonio, 1968.

L-R Rudy Davalos, Tom Nisalke, Spurs Basketball Camp. Edgewood School District student fees paid by Hemphill-McCombs Ford, 1972.

Red and Charline, Johnson City Ranch, 1978.

Red McCombs and Lloyd Brinkman, partners in Brangus cattle.

Charline addressing crowd at longhorn sale, McCombs Ranch, Johnson City, 1984.

Charline and Gladys McCombs (Red's mother), longhorn sale at Johnson City.

Part of the Red McCombs Texas longhorn herd at the Johnson City Ranch, early 1990s.

McCombs takes the mike at one of his Texas long-horn cattle sales—Johnson City, 1987.

Riding Rosa Rockette, 1990.

Red and Charline, Johnson City Ranch, 1980.

L-R James Michener, McCombs and Marty Wender. Michener took a helicopter tour of the McCombs Ranch while researching his book Texas.

Redmac Beau Butler, McCombs' Ranch longhorn herd sire. Bred and raised by Red McCombs, sold for $1 million—an all-time record.

"RM" brand on one of the McCombs' Ranch longhorn cattle.

Bill Forney, left, discusses well in Charline Field with Red, 1985.

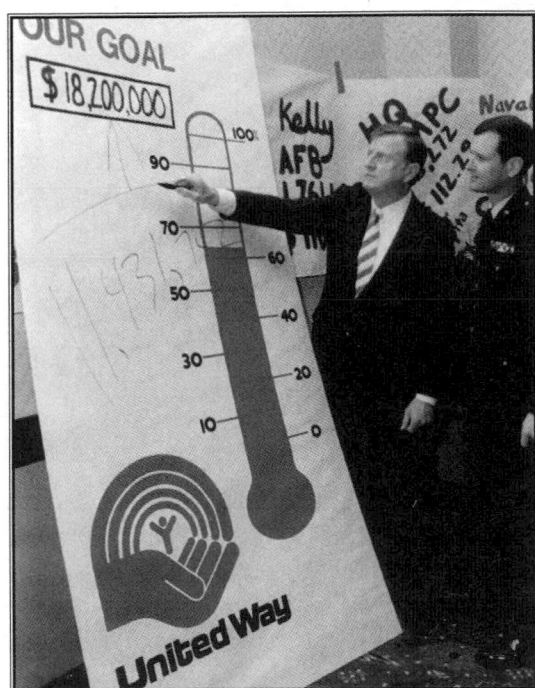

1987—United Way fund drive,
McCombs as chairman. (Below)
Red and Charline announcing
his purchase (re-purchase) of the
Spurs, circa 1988.

—Photo courtesy the
San Antonio Express-News

McCombs with Admiral Staser Holcombe presenting McCombs with drawing after McCombs' finish of most successful United Way fund drive, 1987.

With Mayor Lila Cockrell, 1989.

L-R Red McCombs, Spurs coach Larry Brown, San Antonio mayor Henry Cisneros, at Spurs rally at North Star Mall in San Antonio, welcoming Brown as new coach, 1988.

McCombs being honored— Spurs 25th anniversary, 1997.

McCombs and Gary Woods, 1998.

L-R Rad Weaver (in background), Red McCombs, and Bill Ford at Lions Stadium, October 1999.

Red McCombs in Minnesota, 1999.

McCombs addresses crowd at Vikes training camp in Mankato, 1998.

Red and John Madden at Jets Stadium, September 1999.

Red leads Metrodome in Purple Pride Cheer.

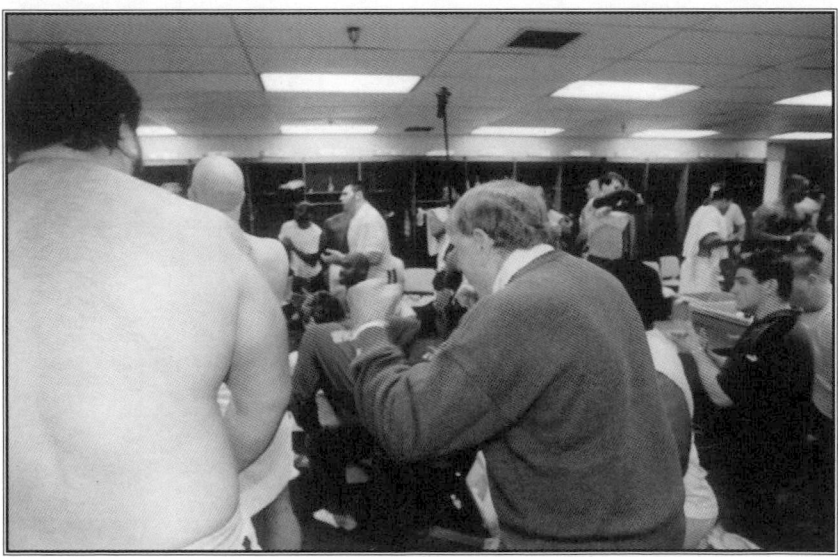

Pep talk to Vikings in dressing room.

Fans at Metrodome, December 1999.

Red, Charline, and Stephen Jones prior to Vikes/Cowboys game.

McCombs and Jerry Jones visit prior to game, 1999.

Red greets Dwayne Rudd after game.

Red and Korey Stringer after Vikings win.

McCombs and Dennis Green after Viking victory over Green Bay.

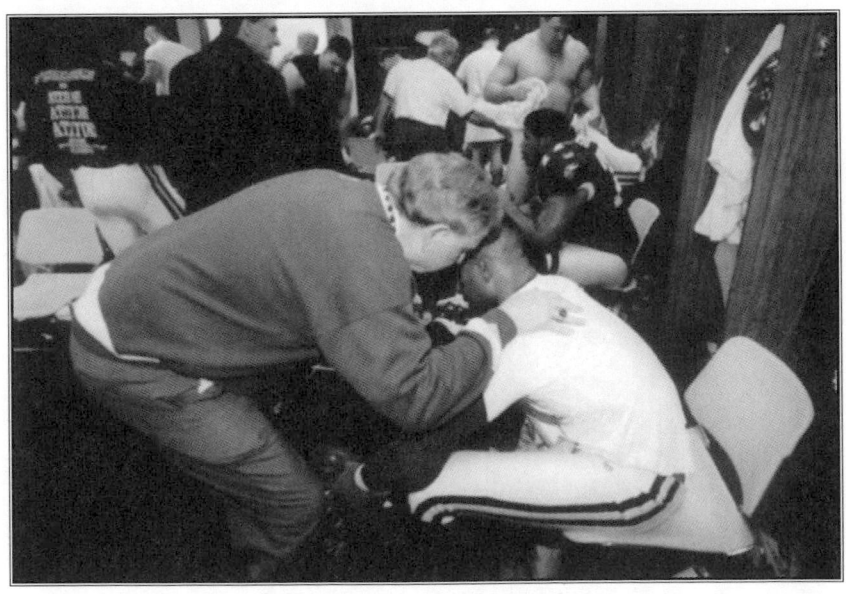

Red consoles Cris Carter after loss.

Red McCombs, Dennis Green, Bill Walsh, prior to Vikes win over 49ers, 1999.

McCombs with Jeff George, 1999.

Charline presented with game ball from Vikings/Cowboys game when Vikes won 27-17, November 1999—#37 Jimmie Hitchcock, Charline, and #81 Chris Walsh.

McCombs hosts hospital kids.

Charline hugs #33 Harold Morrow after game.

McCombs family, Texas Stadium in Dallas, Thanksgiving 1998. Vikes won 42-24.

Charline and Red McCombs Women's Softball Field at University of Texas at Austin.

McCombs and Dan Rather. Rather gave keynote address at the kickoff of Southwestern University's $75 million campaign, which McCombs chaired, 1995.

L-R John Williams, Alan Feld, Lowry Mays, Ted Straus, and Red McCombs. Board of Directors, Clear Channel Communications, 1992.

McCombs with Dr. Mickey LeMaistre and Randy Meyer, M.D. Anderson Cancer Center Annual Meeting, November 1995.

M.D. Anderson Cancer Center Executive Committee, 1995, Red McCombs as chairman (President Bush at left, next to McCombs).

Governor George Bush signing M.D. Anderson legislation, February 1995.

Red and Governor George Bush, July 1991.

Red with Alan Sparger, Jr. at the Westin Galleria (Houston), 1984.

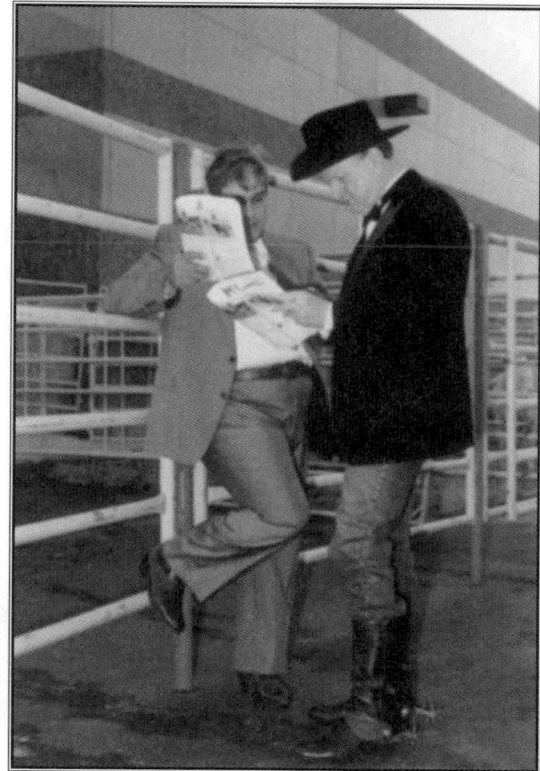

With Sally Pillsbury at University of Minnesota Women's Athletic Department Gala, 1999.

With Jerry Jeff Walker, Texas Two Step Gala in Minnesota, May 5, 1999.

Charline rings Salvation Army Christmas Kettle Bell in Minneapolis, December 1999.

Jenny Dominguez and McCombs at police memorial dedication, police academy, January 1997.

Charline receives honorary doctorate, Southwestern University, May 1997.

Red receives honorary doctorate, Southwestern University, May 1997.

McCombs Christmas family photo, 1995.

Red McCombs in his office, 1999.
—Photo courtesy J.D. Talasek

Red McCombs Automotive Dealership on IH-10, early 1990s.

Red displaying his Dealer Business *Top 100 Mega Dealers magazine cover, 1995.*

Incarnate Word High School seniors say thanks to Red McCombs for bringing back local students stranded at the Olympics, summer 1996.

Red McCombs treats Mary Hull Elementary Students to a day at the San Antonio Zoo, 1997.

Charline and Red at Meadowlands, December 26, 1999. Vikings defeat the Giants.

McCombs family, 1999. Top: L-R Sandy McNab (son-in-law), McCombs, Marsha Shields (daughter). Middle: Ian McNab (grandson), Connie McNab (daughter) Charline, Joseph Shields (grandson). Bottom row: Lynda McCombs (daughter), Sita and Easton McNab (grandchildren). (Below) McCombs family, 2000.

CHAPTER 7

TRAVELS WITH CHARLIE

One of the true tests of friendship is when you push someone into an investment they never wanted, and they don't resent it when the deal winds up making a lot of money. Some people hate feeling obligated.

No two people could have been better friends or less alike. Charlie Thomas is compact, trim, tidy, quiet, reserved, soft-spoken, modest, a man with very little packaging. Charlie has brown, curly hair and looks a little like Bob Dylan. I'm big. I live big. I enjoy people, don't mind crowds. When I'm in a good mood, the normal force of my voice can frighten the birds off the Trinity River. I have tousled red hair, and people say I look like Grizzly Adams, without the beard.

If the weather forecast is partly cloudy, Charlie will carry a raincoat, a hat, and an umbrella. I'll have sunglasses in my shirt pocket.

We met in Corpus Christi in 1956, when I stopped by

a Dodge franchise he managed looking for new car trade-ins. It didn't take a minute to size him up: he was bright, honest, and committed to the long hours the business required. If you kicked his tires, the fender wouldn't fall off.

I tried to hire him on the spot, but the company had made promises to convince him to move to Texas. The promises went unmet—their mistake, my good fortune. A few months later, he quit, called my office and said, "I'm ready to take that offer. If you can pick me up right now, I'll be standing on the corner with my briefcase." He was out of there.

As I expanded, Charlie went from being a general manager to my partner. We bought a bunch of dealerships together and in time he bought his own. The fates were kind, bringing Charlie Thomas into my circle at a crucial period.

I had been awarded the first Edsel dealership in America, quite a coup for a young fellow in a small town in Texas. After two years of prepping, Ford was unveiling the car in September of 1957. With Charlie at my side, along with three of the best salesmen in Corpus Christi, my Edsel franchise immediately recorded the highest volume in the state. Alas, the profits were minimal.

The public was fascinated with the car, which had as much publicity as any model in history. But it reminded me of the advertising agency that created a dynamite campaign for a new dog food. The cans flew off the shelves, and every supermarket clamored for reorders. This time they gathered dust, and the groceries were stuck with cases piled to the ceiling.

"What happened?" the devastated ad agency cried out. "The public loved our campaign."

"Yeah," said the grocers, "but the dogs wouldn't eat the dog food."

But there is no need to rehash the sordid details. I did not like selling people a car they didn't want. The Ford

Motor Company thought I was just a brash young character who lacked the maturity to understand that in this business you had to adjust to certain cycles. They could not believe what I was telling them: I wasn't going to stay with it and they needed to find a dealer to replace us.

In five months, Charlie and I went back to my two used car lots, and I learned a life lesson. You have to know the difference between a slump and a situation that is hopeless. Custer did not have a slump at Little Big Horn.

Charlie was settled in Houston, and had all or a piece of twenty dealerships in the Southwest, when I received a phone call from Sidney Shlenker, a man with interesting contacts. Sidney was the son of a prominent Houston banker. He once worked for Judge Roy Hofheinz, the visionary who built the Astrodome, and had co-founded a company called Pace Management to produce sports and show business events across the country. One of their undertakings was the hit Broadway musical "Best Little Whorehouse in Texas."

Sidney was calling to tip me off that the Houston Rockets were on the block, and the Maloof family might be conducting a fire sale. Sidney had no way of knowing that I was within two days of purchasing the Denver Nuggets. And a few years later, Shlenker would buy them from me. But for now, his interest was in acquiring a share of the Rockets, if the right majority buyer could be found.

I said, "I can't do it, but I know someone who would be ideal." I called Ray Patterson, the general manager, who was handling the details. The Rockets had a rather curious history. They were the only team in the NBA that changed owners more frequently than coaches. There had been five in ten years, and Ray had worked for the last four. The team could be bought for less than $10 million.

I called Charlie at his car dealership, told him the price, and said flatly, "You need to buy this team."

He said, "Why are you even talking about this?

Owning a basketball team is the last thing I want to do. That's your thing. I'm not into sports. I'm not a public person. Hell, Red, you know me. I'm a car man."

"Charlie, we're not talking about privacy or even about sports. We're talking about making money."

He raised all the basic objections that I knew he would. And I bombarded him with all of my arguments. The NBA was on the verge of a huge network television contract and a national marketing boom (although no one could have imagined the heights it would reach in the 1990s).

I thought the Rockets were respectable, and maybe one move away from being a very good team. They had reached the finals in 1980 with a club that finished under .500 but got hot in the stretch. Moses Malone was an all-star center and the previous year's most valuable player.

Moses was a free agent, but Patterson, a very discreet guy, assured me they would sign him to a new contract and had made allowances for it in the budget.

I told the doubting Thomas that I saw the purchase of the Rockets as a bargain. With the sport about to explode, it was a chance to make a fortune. When I had him thinking of it as a long-term investment, and not a daily headache, he was ready to check out the books.

On the day I closed on the Nuggets, it was announced that Charlie Thomas intended to buy the Rockets. I was thrilled that my friend and I would share in this timely venture, and the friendly rivalry that was an implied part of any sports package.

Within days after the sale had gone through, Charlie reached me at my desk. He was beside himself. "Red," he said, "the worst thing that I could have contemplated has already happened. I've got every telephone line at my dealership tied up with sports nuts. TV camera crews and newspaper reporters are camped outside my door."

"What in the world for?" I asked, innocently enough. I had not heard any news out of Houston, certainly not that

Moses Malone had signed a $13 million contract with the Philadelphia 76ers.

Quickly, Charlie gave me the highlights. "Apparently," he said, "Ray miscalculated on what Moses would do. They have already held a press conference in Philadelphia. Harold Katz (the owner) posed with Moses, holding up a 76er jersey. He's our best player, the only one we have who is in his prime, and now we've lost him. What am I going to do?"

My brain started whirling. "Charlie," I said, "you have fifteen days under the rules to match that offer." From what he had said, I gathered that when reporters raised that question Katz said it was not an issue. "Charlie, you may have just won the lottery."

I was referring to the lottery for the first pick in the draft. The other kind, the pick sixes, were not yet in vogue in so many states.

Thomas said, "What do you mean?"

"If the contract is drawn in any way to prohibit you from matching their offer, you won't have to deal with Mr. Katz. The commissioner (David Stern) will take care of that. Your move is to invite the media into your office and tell them you are delighted to see that other clubs appreciate the value of Moses. And no matter what the terms, you reserve your right to match them."

"How do I know I want to do that?"

"You don't," I said, "but you have fifteen days to think about it. If you decide not to do it, you just say you plan to run the team in a responsible way and you are not going to bust the budget. But the longer you delay, the more you're likely to get in return from the 76ers."

In the end, that was the way it played out. Katz gave up Caldwell Jones, a seven-foot center, and his 1983 first draft pick, for the rights to Malone. Moses went on to win a ring in Philadelphia and to finish his career by being voted one of the NBA's fifty greatest players.

His was a remarkable story. Moses was the first major player to sign with the pros directly out of high school, joining Virginia in the ABA. When the league dissolved, he went to Buffalo, only to be traded to Houston in October of 1976.

Moses wasn't much of a talker and rarely smiled, but he came up with one very profound line. Asked the biggest difference he had found in making the jump from high school to pro ball, he replied, "In high school, the players are younger."

It was hard, if not impossible, for Charlie Thomas to see any advantage in Malone's departure. How people react to getting a blessing in disguise depends on how thorough the disguise is.

But without Moses, the Rockets finished last the next two seasons, and Charlie won both coin tosses, enabling the team to draft Ralph Sampson and Hakeem Olajuwon in consecutive seasons. With Philly's draft pick, they selected Rodney McCray, a good NBA player whose career was dogged by injuries.

Actually, it was Charlie's angels, his wife Kittsie and the youngest of his three daughters, Tracy, who called the coin tosses. Still, when they write "The History of the Coin Flip in America," the Thomases will rate at least a couple of paragraphs.

Since I had been the one who pushed him into becoming an NBA owner, I could not be more proud of his eleven years at the helm of the Rockets. He used the same basic common sense he employed as a car dealer to a business that is fundamentally insane. And he left behind the key player, Olajuwon, the coach, Rudy Tomjanovich, and the core of a team that won two NBA champions for the next owner, Les Alexander.

Charlie may have set a record when he went ten years pretty much without attracting heavy media criticism or rioting by the fans. He had stayed out of the spotlight, faithfully attending the games and trying not to block anyone's view when he and Kittsie leaped to their feet to scold a referee.

We remained the closest of friends, in every way, but it got very competitive. We couldn't sit together when my Denver or San Antonio teams played Houston. Whenever my team won, he insisted the officials had robbed them.

In 1992 the team was struggling, and he concluded that he had to fire a coach he liked, Don Chaney. Hakeem's feelings were hurt over the issue of renegotiating his contract, and the jewel of Nigeria had demanded a trade.

The fans and press were taking sides, as they usually do, and really for the first time Thomas found himself catching heat. Other owners, and a few in the media, assured him that it was time to trade Olajuwon. This is the NBA way. When your superstar is judged as too temperamental, the cry goes up to unload him.

But to his credit, Charlie had figured out a few angles. "I've learned one thing about this game," he said. "It's talent-driven. And Hakeem is a great talent. I'm going to wait him out."

Which he did. Hakeem stayed, signed a new contract, and everyone kissed and made up. In Houston's two championship seasons he was the most valuable player, taking apart the league's other great centers along the way— David Robinson, Patrick Ewing, and Shaquille O'Neal.

By anyone's standards, Thomas was a quality owner who gave his city very little grief. By his fourth season, he had broken the longevity record for a Rockets owner. He did not give the press colorful phrases, but when he said something there was often a nice bite to it. He was certainly sincere when he said he appreciated all the coverage the Rockets received.

"It's the only free advertising I ever get," he said. "If I wanted to advertise one of my cars, you wouldn't even say it was a bad one for free."

When he sold the team to Alexander, and the Rockets

went on to win the world titles in 1994 and 1995, he was asked if he had any regrets, any second thoughts. "No," he said, quite honestly. "I'm a car dealer. When a customer drives off my lot and he feels like he's got a great deal, then I'm happy. That's how I want him to feel."

Charlie didn't make out badly on the sale price, either. It was reported to be $85 million.

I talked him into buying the Rockets around the same time I bought the Nuggets. And, by coincidence, we sold our franchises (I had repurchased the Spurs) in the same year, in 1993.

You suspect he left with at least a twinge of regret. We all do. I've said it before: of all the things I've done in my life, nothing makes the adrenaline flow like owning a sports team.

The argument is ageless concerning how essential the owner is to a winning franchise, other than to sign the checks. And many employ an accountant to handle even that responsibility.

Offhand, you look at baseball, where George Steinbrenner in New York, Ted Turner in Atlanta, and Marge Schott in Cincinnati were each suspended from active ownership with no dramatic difference in the team's performance. But I do believe that attitude as well as a sense of direction is critical to the success of a team. These do start at the top.

A guy giving up a franchise is like the patient whose doctor advised him to give up drinking, smoking, and women. "Will I live longer?" he asked.

"No," said the doctor, "but it will seem like it."

Charlie left pro basketball richer in spirit and purse than when he came in. And I can only take pleasure in that.

CHAPTER 8

INSURING THE WORLD

I think of striped trousers, top hats and tails, and men with mutton chop sideburns and walking sticks with gold caps. I hear the bell tolling, as people scurry through the great hall, as they did in an age when pirates cruised the seas and no merchant ship was safe.

In my imagination, this is how I once saw Lloyd's of London, who have insured everything from the *Titanic* to Betty Grable's legs to Dolly Parton's bosom.

Now, I am not certain about Dolly, but I have no doubt that the idea was discussed because a friend of mine asked what kind of coverage would be involved: "Accident or collision?"

Captains and kings and ordinary people have thought and talked about Lloyd's since the seventeenth century. In the early 1970s, I happened to read a book about the company and I was fascinated by the history of it. In brief, the story line is this: Three hundred years ago, merchants in

England sold their goods to merchants in Venice, but the pirates controlled the seas.

In 1668 a conversation took place in Earl Lloyd's coffee shop that would change the way the world did business. One merchant happened to mention that he had received a very nice order from Venice, but it was payable only on delivery. Since he could not guarantee that it would ever arrive, he lamented, how could he accept the risk of filling the order?

A gentleman spoke up and asked, "How much would you pay me if I guaranteed that order?"

So began what became a regular practice. A statement of a ship's cargo would be read aloud. Among the coffee house patrons, those who were willing to share the loss, if the cargo disappeared, signed their names below the list.

From that small conversation grew one of society's most revered institutions, but one we take today rather matter-of-factly. A second point caught my interest. Although at risk for billions of dollars, Lloyd's had a business plan that did not include capital that would come anywhere close to covering potential losses. From the day it was founded in a London coffee shop, the company essentially has used as its capital the honor and good name of its shareholders, who are called members, as if they belonged to a very privileged club, which indeed they do.

I was more or less smitten by the idea that this company everyone knows, that had played such a huge role in building a worldwide commerce, was in the 1970s still underwritten by the pledge of each member to surrender his entire net worth if called upon to do so.

The story so intrigued me that I contacted Lloyd's of London and spoke with one David Coles, who was the representative of several underwriters. We began the process of my becoming a member, or as one is sometimes referred to, a "name" of Lloyd's. As I casually mentioned this possibility to my associates, I could not contain my enthusiasm. The thought exhilarated me.

In turn, they looked at me with disbelief and said, "You are begging to be a part of a company where you commit your total net worth?" I said yes, that is the element that excites me. Of course, I understood why this impulse tends to make lawyers and accountants nervous.

Why I need this sort of stimulation, I can no more explain than others can describe the allure of climbing a mountain. Frostbite? Avalanche? Snow-blindness? Let's go! You bring the beer. I don't do mountains. But in my lifetime, I have on occasion found it hard to resist a proposition that gives me a chance to go broke.

After two years of submitting records and processing papers, I received the phone call I had been waiting for like a lovesick teenager. "Mr. McCombs," I was told, "you will now select from the following dates to meet with the committee that makes the final decision."

At the time, Lloyd's consisted of 270 syndicates, insuring hundreds of different types of programs. I had applied to be part of a program that insured workmen's comp, the airlines, and maritime losses. The schedules of the syndicates are as varied as life itself.

My investment was a minimal amount of capital for a share in the annual profits. As a return on cash, historically, it was phenomenal. That was not my primary motivation, although I did not ignore it. The real advantage to me was belonging to a unique society, the only one whose balance sheet was to a large extent the honor and bond and word of its members-slash-names.

Yet when David Coles called, I could not resist trying a bit of gamesmanship, even though I knew in advance what his answer would be. I decided to pull a typical Red McCombs, push-the-limits ploy. I explained to Mr. Coles that I would be accompanied by my wife, Charline, who also would join me at the meeting.

In a superior, Clifton Webb tone of voice, he responded,

"Mr. McCombs, no one goes before the committee except the candidate."

I explained to him that Texas was a community property state. I was testing him, of course. As I expected, his reaction was totally negative. "David," I said, one good ole boy to another, "everyone has a boss. You go talk to yours because this is a deal breaker." It was not, but he agreed to consult his boss, although clearly not happy about it.

When he called back, he said that the policy was as he stated and he regretted that both parties had spent two years in this process in vain. He would be returning my materials and documents promptly, and he sounded sincere when he said he was sorry it had not worked out.

I said, "Aw, hell, if they're going to be ornery about it, I'll just give in and make the trip anyway." I don't know what I would have done if they had said, "Sure, bring your wife." I just wanted to see if I could bend a rule. The last thing Charline wanted was to sit through one more committee meeting.

We flew to London, took in the sights, and then toured the elderly Lloyd's building, where the walls reflected an unending admiration and debt to the Royal Navy. Davey Jones, Lord Nelson, and the other naval heroes of long ago ultimately rid them of the pirates. I soaked it all in—the magnificent paintings, the use of the big ledger, the storied bell that rang in the event of a calamity. Even in this day of modern technology, if a calamity occurs it is entered into the ledger by hand and a quill pen, dipped in an inkwell. No one surpasses the British at carrying on a tradition.

We were treated to a private luncheon with the leaders of Lloyd's and the committee that would judge me. At lunch, I realized I was short on cash and we were leaving the next day to spend a couple of weeks traveling in Europe. I turned to David Coles, mentioned that I needed $5,000, and said Charline would write them a check while I was going before the committee.

While there was a nodding of heads, and nothing was said about that request, I sensed that something was askew. When I left to go with my sponsor, there was a noticeable amount of whispering and ducking in and out of rooms. Finally, I was told that the banks were closed and Lloyd's doesn't keep cash. I found that comical. Doesn't keep cash. They were able to get a bank to open, and Charline cashed the check.

The board room was at least ninety feet long, with two conference tables, ten chairs on one side, and a single chair for the candidate on the other. The scene was quite imposing, but it was a very simple interview. Quickly, they asked if I understood that I was signing over my net worth according to English law, forfeiting any rights I might have under U.S. law. The underwriter would have the authority to bind me to any kind of insurance program he saw fit, with absolutely no input from me.

I had already accepted these conditions in a lawyer's office, but they wanted to confirm that I had a full understanding of these terms. My advance to them was something like $150,000, but I was agreeing to bind my potential loss to my entire net worth. They asked me if I had any reservations about this obligation.

I believe they were surprised by my reaction. I was clearly enjoying myself. I asked them if any candidate had ever gone to this level and decided not to proceed. They said, yes, very rarely, but it did happen, usually because of heirs becoming members and the liability being passed on.

My second question was, "Do you have women who are members?" The answer was yes. It had been a men's club for two or three centuries, but had grown more tolerant in recent years. They had not admitted members from outside the United Kingdom until 1968.

I knew all I needed to know. With the stroke of a pen, I bound over my entire net worth to the good judgment of Lloyd's of London.

The excitement I felt personally from this decision overwhelmed any concerns I might have had. The reality of losing one's wealth had not been a significant item in the history of Lloyd's. Sadly, it is now. Lawsuits that were initiated by U.S. members, and ongoing for eight years, wiped out family fortunes here and among some of the grand names of England and Europe. Some had been members for 300 years. But Lloyd's has suffered losses beyond anything they had forecast.

So how did Red fare in what I still regard as the deal with the most class of any I ever made? I was lucky to get in and lucky to get out.

In the mid-1980s, while I was in Denver on business related to my ownership of the Nuggets, I read a small item on the business page. A company had been held liable for a man's health problems attributed to the use of asbestos in ships that were built in California in 1940 and 1941. It was a small story that escalated into a huge story with grave consequences. Johns Mansville was among the first of several large manufacturers to declare bankruptcy.

At the time, I don't recall the small story that I spotted in the Denver paper received much attention across the country. But my intuition kicked in. (If a hunch turns out to be right, this is referred to as having "vision.") A man had been awarded millions in damages because of a product used forty years earlier. That was a red flag. Unrealistic tort claims were probably going to become the order of the day in the United States.

At that point, I notified Lloyd's that I was resigning, which you are allowed to do. Your obligation has a tail of three years. In my case, it turned out to be eight because of the lawsuits filed in the U.S. attacking the unlimited liability of the standard agreement. A lot of those who sued did get some recourse and did not lose their entire estate.

But there were staggering losses, particularly in the United Kingdom, where members saw their income stream shut off, and many had their property foreclosed to pay off debts.

I am not making a judgment on those who sued. What comes to mind is a line from a Woody Allen movie: "Life is like Las Vegas. You're up. You're down. In the end, the house always wins. That doesn't mean you didn't have fun."

For me, the bottom line was that I suffered no loss. I had the personal fulfillment and pride of knowing I had been involved in the most unusual business concept in the world. And I had the good luck, or foresight, to not overstay my visit.

Out of that trip to London came another of life's pleasures: an exposure to the marvels of Europe. Beginning in the early 1970s, we began to vacation there from time to time.

Among other things, the trips fed my passion for collecting. As a collector, I rank somewhere between avid and obsessed. Over the years, I have gone from antique ivory to precious silver to Texana, western Americana, Indian artifacts, antique guns. I have all but jumped out of boots at getting a call from a broker saying he has a piece dated 1690, or finding in a country store a journal that reported General Custer and his troops were leaving in a week on a patrol that would take them to Little Big Horn.

I spent fifteen years chasing a Gatling gun with its full encasement, platform, and carriage, then bought not one but two. I would have bought a dozen. The thrill is in realizing that the prize has been worth the chase.

I don't consider myself an expert on anything I collect. My system is to look at an item and decide what my level of interest is. If that exceeds the price, then I buy. My purchases are not always prudent, but I never intended to sell them anyway. There is one duty that I believe strongly applies to collectibles: you should share them with the public when opportunities arise. This I try to do.

When I first started to collect silver, we were nearing

the end of a two-week family driving tour of Ireland. Charline and myself and our daughters Lynda and Connie ended up in Dublin one afternoon, and the girls had plans that didn't include me.

With time on my hands, I wandered into the hotel lobby to buy a fine cigar to smoke in the park. I was paying for my cigar when I noticed a paperback on the joys of collecting antique Irish silver. I sat down and began to leaf through the book. According to the author, Irish silversmiths were not to be considered superior to others of their time. There were so few of them, and such little demand in such a poor country, that all of this had converged to make Irish silver rarer than most.

I was intrigued by this, and asked the concierge for directions to the nearest shop. They had several pieces, among them two beautifully matched soup tureens. I had no knowledge of what a fair price would be—a distinct disadvantage in such matters. So befuddled, but intrigued, I found myself going back to the shop and trying to barter with the owner. I made some headway, then ran into a dead end. He wanted $7,000-8,000 for the set. He would not budge. There was no more headway to be gained.

The four of us were in the car with our driver, ready to leave Dublin, and I was still complaining about the high-priced antique Irish silver, and what a ripoff I thought it was.

Connie, my fourteen-year-old, interrupted me. "Daddy," she said, wearily, "you must be the most stupid man who ever lived."

My self-esteem has taken an occasional dip, but I thought this assessment might be a trifle harsh. I said, "Well, Connie, share your thoughts with me."

She continued, "For three days you have bored us to tears with how much you loved those two stupid soup tureens. Why didn't you just buy them and spare us all this misery?"

My answer was, "I thought the price was too high." And in my daughter's eyes I could read the message: "Here is a man who can afford to buy something he wants, and he doesn't like the price given him by a person who does this as a profession."

I told the driver to turn the car around, and I went back into the shop and bought the two soup tureens. We still have them. And in case you were thinking this story would come full circle, it doesn't. I insure my collectibles with a company in San Antonio.

CHAPTER 9

RED ALERT

I made one of my larger mistakes by not buying the Houston Astros in the late 1970s, when the club could have been bought at a bargain basement price. During part of that time, I was too busy to chase the deal. I was in a hospital trying real hard not to die.

Darrell Royal, who learned just about all he needed to know during the Oklahoma Dust Bowl, went on to become a championship football coach at the University of Texas. Mental toughness, common sense, and wit were the Royal trademarks, and he shared them with his friends. Darrell once found himself pondering a statement by Oliver Wendell Holmes. The late chief justice of the Supreme Court had been quoted as saying that if he discovered a secret formula for avoiding the afflictions and misery and grief of everyday life, he would not reveal it because people need to be tested and to overcome adversity.

"That struck me as profound," said Royal, "and I gave

it a lot of thought. What I finally concluded was, piss on Oliver Wendell Holmes."

I understood how Darrell felt. He is one of the least selfish people I have ever met. But most of us need to be tested. I know I was.

In my forty-eighth year, I realized I had a problem with alcohol. I've had people ask me how you can tell when you need to stop drinking, and my answer is a simple one. You know you have a problem when you can't get through the day without it.

I didn't drink at all until I was twenty. Up to then I had been trying to develop as an athlete, but even so I was not your typical twenty-year-old. I began to drink socially, at a fairly steady clip, from the time I was twenty-five. Gradually, it became a little bit more of a necessity. The need sneaks up on you, which is why this illness can be so hard to confront. Another is the fact that drinking is traditionally a kind of American sport, legal and acceptable and all too available.

When I was around forty-seven, I began to challenge myself to see if I could go several days at a time without a drink. I found that it was virtually impossible to do so, and that bothered me greatly—although not enough to stop, or even cut back. An addiction to chemicals is hard for anyone to fully understand if they haven't been through one. Most of the people I have known who were addicted to booze were able to hide it pretty well. But they had to become liars and sneaks to live with their habit. In my vernacular, instead of becoming falling down drunk, they stayed half drunk all the time.

But the damage to your health catches up with you, even if the problem never reaches the proportions of Ray Milland in the movie *Lost Weekend,* with bottles hidden in the light fixtures. I don't think I ever became mean or unruly or passed out with my head in a spittoon. I had enough discipline to build and maintain a multimillion-dollar enterprise. I didn't like the way I felt. My system had to be fed. It was like feeding a python.

In my case, God decided to handle the problem for me. I went into a convulsive state one morning at home, and Charline thought I was having a stroke. In fact, I had experienced an attack of hepatitis, magnified by my overuse of alcohol. I don't remember the ambulance ride to the hospital in San Antonio. I was unconscious and unaware for several days, and Charline made the decision to have me moved to Methodist Hospital in Houston.

After my hepatitis had been diagnosed, the doctors asked her if Mr. McCombs had a drinking problem. She replied, quite honestly, no, she didn't think so, "but he does drink a lot."

The first few days, Charline was told bluntly that the odds were against my survival. Then they told her a miracle was happening. I would survive, but would be dependent on a dialysis machine. Then they said I was facing a long period of recovery, but I would not be on dialysis. "There are complications," they said, in a message intended for me. "He has a surprisingly healthy liver."

Once I was conscious, and praying constantly, I began to come out of the fog. After eight days in the hospital, my mind had cleared and I no longer had a craving for alcohol. That may sound glib, too quick or too easy, but it was true. My body had been detoxed. I asked a doctor the best way to be sure I could quit drinking. He said different people try different cures. Some join Alcoholics Anonymous. Others check into clinics and go through rehab. Still others withdraw from their friends and society. None of the ways are easy.

My hospital stay, and the physical crisis I survived, had gotten me through the hard part. This was a last-resort treatment. I don't recommend it. There are better programs than a near-death experience. I went through the process without joining a twelve-step program. I follow the twelve steps and strongly believe in them. But my recovery came in a different way.

I thanked God for delivering me, and with His help I have been sober for going on twenty-two years. I have not had a drink since November 12, 1977, and I don't plan on ever having another. I would rather blow my brains out. But I do know it is a day-to-day issue.

What I have to stress is that you cannot do this by yourself. This was verified for me by my doctors, after my release, when I came back for a series of weekly tests. I was told that they had treated many patients who had died from conditions not as severe as mine. My recovery could be attributed to three factors: 1) excellent medical technology; 2) a highly motivated patient, and 3) a power greater than any of us.

I was blessed by that power and consider it an absolute truth. I can't say this any plainer: God intended for me to do other things.

All of the above explains, in part, why I didn't jump when the Houston Astros were being shopped in 1977. By then, Judge Roy Hofheinz, the visionary who built the world's first indoor stadium, had suffered a stroke and had gradually lost the ballclub and other properties to the Ford and General Electric credit companies. Everyone was eager for a sale. It is rare when players and fans feel any warmth toward an owner. It is impossible to hug a credit company.

The franchise and the real estate could be bought for around $10 million, a price below the market, but no local buyers were clamoring to take on the judge's faded empire. The Astros were a last-place team, and the Astrodome was in a state of some disrepair.

Owning our minor league club in Corpus Christi had been one of the best times of my life, and I was not immune to the big league label. Over the next eighteen months, the Astros were still on the block. My interest in the deal began to pick up, and my health and energy had been restored. But not for long.

Just as everything might have come together, a doctor discovered a complication with one of my kidneys, unrelated to my earlier ordeal. The surgery involved an incision that went from the belly button to the backbone, and while the convalescence was not a long one I had begun to get that picked-on feeling. I was in and out of the hospital in late July, and Charline thought I needed a change of scenery. She suggested that we fly to Aspen on our Lear jet.

The doctors said I could set my own pace, and after a few days in Aspen I began to get antsy. I started to think about buying another ranch.

From the time we married, Charline had indicated to me many times that she would like to own a small ranch in the Texas Hill Country, west of Austin. Now, I need to explain that her image of a ranch had no close connection to what a ranch really is. Hers was a Hollywood image, the Ponderosa with a large garden. I had grown up in ranch country and knew that running one was hard, grueling work accompanied by occasional heartache. But while I was recovering from my bout with hepatitis in 1978, Charline would take me on drives into the Hill Country. Very shortly, we didn't have a little ranch. We owned a 5,000-acre spread south of Johnson City.

I definitely caught the ranching fever, and decided the best way to see the West was to charter a small plane. I could land at each stop and a broker would meet the plane and take me on a tour. Charline thought I had lost my mind. But it was a great way to see the American West, the Rocky Mountains, the painted desert, and the Badlands. I spent a month traveling across Colorado, Wyoming, Utah, Montana, some of the Dakotas. We fell in love with an area of Colorado, where we now have a ranch and a home that fill a meaningful role in our lives.

This is what is known as the Law of Unintended

Consequences. I am not certain we would have wound up in the cattle business, at all, if I had not twice felt a need to relax and rebuild my strength.

Starting in Johnson City, my plan was to stock that ranch with longhorn cattle because of my interest in Texas history. I knew that Charlie Schreiner, of the legendary YO Ranch, and Happy Shahan, in Brackettville, had longhorn herds. Charlie turned me over to his son, Walter, who became one of my closest friends. What I found out very quickly was how narrow the price spread was between the best cattle and the ones graded as merely good. But no one wanted to sell their best cattle.

I found a young man named Alan Sparger, whose father owned a large herd at Hondo. Alan, who owned a smaller one, was like a living encyclopedia of Texas longhorn cattle. He knew every breed. Suddenly, while flying over ranches all day, a light came on and I knew what I needed to do. If the top cattle were so hard to buy, why didn't I create a market? All I had to do was overpay and build up my own herd.

It was possible to buy a mediocre pair of longhorns, a cow and a calf, for $750. I started making offers of $1,500 and $2,000 a pair, and the ranchers started selling to me. I fell in love with this idea of creating a market. I told Alan I wanted to stage a large sale and bring in people from all over the country. He tried mightily to discourage me. The idea was frivolous, he said. I had been in the business for less than eight months. I would be known as a trader, not a true cattleman, which was roughly the difference between a pimp and an art collector.

I ignored his advice and held the sale. We sold 150 cattle, losing money on many of them. But when it was over, I had in one day created a new market and attracted buyers from sixteen states.

From that first one, in 1978, through 1990, I staged two auctions a year for twelve years. I copyrighted the phrase "The Texas Legacy Sale," and started the first Tux and Boots Cattle Sale in Houston. In the ballroom of the fancy Westin Galleria Hotel, we staged a sale of Texas longhorn cattle, covered by the national media, including the *New York Times* and the *Los Angeles Times*. We charged a hundred dollars a head just to get in the door, sold out every affair, and gave that money to charity. The longhorns not only were back as a breed—they were back with a vengeance. By the time I staged my last sale, I had raised a bull named Redmac Beau Butler and syndicated him to twenty different breeders for one million dollars. We did it in one day, and the syndication was oversold.

I am not prepared to say that breeding and selling cattle provided me with a kind of therapy, but my life took a definite turn after my two hospital stays. I became much more sensitive about putting limits on what I could or could not do.

In 1986 I visited a longtime friend of mine from Fort Worth who was being treated at the M. D. Anderson Cancer Center in Houston. His prognosis was not good. I was aware of M. D. Anderson's reputation as the most respected facility of its kind in the world, but I had no association with its work. No one in our family had been stricken with cancer. We had been blessed.

There was nothing unusual or unexpected about my visit, but some vague feeling I could not identify tugged at me in the taxi to the airport and on the plane back to San Antonio. Eventually, I brushed it off and my thoughts moved on to other things.

The next week I went back to M. D. Anderson to revisit my friend. As I was greeted by a parking attendant, stopped at the information desk, and went up to the room, it dawned on me what had eluded me the previous visit. I was witnessing one of the most unique approaches to caring and genuine concern I had ever known.

I remembered how, a week earlier, a guest who was visiting the other patient in the room had called out to a nurse as he was leaving. He held out a parking stub and asked, "Can you point me in the right direction? The last time I was here, I got hopelessly lost." The nurse called over a nurse's aid and said, "Would you take this gentleman to his car, please?"

It was a small gesture, I suppose, and one that 90 percent of the visitors to a hospital, who are often distracted, would have missed. But the symbol was huge. These were people who really cared in a practical and attentive way.

After I left the room, I couldn't wait to call Dr. Mickey LeMaistre, someone I had known since the 1960s and a former vice president of the University of Texas. I had lost touch with Mickey, although I knew he had been president of M.D. Anderson for several years. He invited me to stop by his office.

He motioned me to a chair and said, "Glad you're here. We have some catching up to do." I told him how impressed I was with his staff, and he handed me a mission statement which said, simply, "People who enter these doors, the patients and the people who visit them, are troubled. We need to be aware of this and go that extra mile in the care we give."

I told Dr. LeMaistre I had witnessed an example of this service, and I thought it was remarkable, knowing that hospitals function seven days a week, twenty-four hours a day. He did not achieve all the high positions he has filled by being passive. "If you're that interested," he said, "why don't I get you on one of our boards?"

The next thing I knew, I was on the Board of Visitors and was asked to take on a couple of projects. Then, in 1994, he asked me to head up a select committee to study all phases of M.D. Anderson as the hospital prepared itself for the next revolution in health care. That was one of the most significant roles I have ever held, chairing the Institutional Initiatives Committee.

One thing led to another, as they often do. In October of 1995, I was asked to chair the board for two years, succeeding Randy Meyer, who had been the CEO of Exxon. Meanwhile, I was appointed to the steering committee with Ben Love, the respected Houston banker, to raise $150 million in a five-year plan.

At nineteen, Ben had flown a B-17 Flying Fortress on bombing raids over Germany in World War II. It was no big stretch for him to provide the leadership, and we met our goal in half the time allotted in two and a half years.

Dr. Mickey LeMaistre retired in 1996, with a superb legacy in place. I will always be grateful to him for inviting me to get involved with M.D. Anderson. It is one of a kind, and I don't feel I am slighting San Antonio by the time and effort I contribute there. The hospital is a treasure for all Texans, as was intended when the state legislature created it in 1941.

CHAPTER 10

PARTNERS

I do not do Top Ten Lists. I do not plaster my office with slogans or proverbs. I have a few core convictions that guide my business decisions, in addition to the work ethic I learned from my dad.

Of course, we are all shaped to some extent by the environment of our early years. In my case, that would be the town of Spur, in Dickens County, on the high plains between Lubbock and Abilene.

You do not watch people scratch out a living, with pride and dignity, and not come away with some down-home wisdom. A fellow I knew was working once on a construction job, shoveling sand. He was on his last leg by the third day, when an old-timer suggested that he grip the shovel lower and not try to fill it.

"Just get enough sand to be comfortable," he said. "You ain't going to run out of sand." It made the job a lot easier, and the young fellow asked why he hadn't told him the secret the first day. "You wouldn't have believed me the first day," came the reply.

Anyone who ever tried to paint a wall knows there is a mystique to it. Once, as a boy, I kept complaining about the fact that the paint on my brush kept dripping on my nose when I tried to do some edging. A pro finished the job and scolded me gently. "The paint don't go," he said, "except where you put it."

There is a pride and an art all its own to manual labor. One is reminded of the hired hand who was asked how he could seem so lazy and get so much plowing done. "To tell you the truth," he said, "I let the mule do most of it."

These are terrific lessons, and if you are not as dense as a rock you only have to learn them once. You don't have to be humble to succeed, but I don't believe Elmer Fudd sold many vacuum cleaners by hoping no one was home when he knocked on the door.

You do need to be aware that there is no such thing as a self-made man. I'm certainly not one. We all have help along the way. But if you define "self-made" as having created wealth when you were not born with a family fortune, yeah, I have done that.

If I had to reveal only one key condition for success in business, it would be to pick great partners—if partners are necessary. You should pick someone who would put his hand in the fire for you and vice versa. I have been blessed in this realm. The partners I had—or still have—were keepers. This is rare because too often partners end up with one or both being unhappy. I will not take an active position in anyone else's company. The bottom-line responsibility and the bottom-line say-so are what interest me.

My association with Charlie Thomas is described elsewhere in these pages. Here are a few more who enriched my world.

LOWRY MAYS

Sometime in 1972, Lowry Mays, then an investment banker, stopped by my office and said he was brokering the sale of an FM radio station and the deal was not going to close. I don't recall the conversation lasting very long. We decided to do the deal ourselves, and Lowry would try to buy a few other radio stations.

We had known each other since the 1960s, and I had invested with him in a number of joint ventures and limited partnerships. Lowry was a product of Highland Park in Dallas, the school that produced Doak Walker and Bobby Layne. He was a Texas Aggie with a degree in petroleum engineering. After serving in the military, he went to Harvard and got an MBA.

During the first two or three years of the company, Mays kept his "day" job as an investment banker. We had brought in a young man from Dallas, John Barger, to run the radio end of the business—the only end we had at the time. After we found success with another half dozen stations, Lowry looked at the industry and decided he wanted to delve more deeply into the business than we had planned.

I was delighted with that decision because Lowry is an extremely talented guy. This was the first real indication I had that we might build a fairly good-sized regional company. Until then, there was no thought in my mind that we would ever become a huge, international company. My thinking was along familiar lines: do the one deal, buy some assets, increase their value, then sell. We didn't have any timetable or plan to do that. But on a clear day, I didn't see forever. Lowry did—and I give him all the credit for that.

I was there from the "git-go," but Mays built and expanded the company. We took Clear Channel Communications public in 1984, and the growth kicked into a higher gear. In these turbulent times, the numbers change by the month, if not by the week, but Clear Channel at last report was the largest operator of radio stations in the world, with over 1,200, along with 28 television stations. The company had acquired Jacor Communications, AMFM, the radio giant owned by Tom Hicks, and SFX Entertainment. It was number one in the United States in outdoor amphitheaters and second in billboards.

Lowry and his wife, Peggy, a San Antonio girl, have four children, and sons Mark and Randall hold leadership positions in the company.

Mays has served as a regent on the Texas A&M board, as chair of the Chamber of Commerce and the United Way, and is a past chairman of the National Association of Broadcasters. He is a member of the Texas Business Hall of Fame and has been recognized by his peers multiple times.

I remember Lowry calling me many years ago and asking me to pick out a date the next week when I could fly to Louisville with him. We were interested in buying a chain of radio stations, and I believe the number he used was $20 million. My response was, "Lowry, you're not talking about radio. You must be talking about television stations." He said no, these were radio stations, but they represented a large portion of that very good market and had been in the same family's hands since their inception.

I went to Louisville with him and we closed the deal. We have never had a disagreeable word between us. He is the chairman of the board and CEO of Clear Channel. I'm a director, and even with the jolts Wall Street has suffered, my stock in the company is still the largest holding in all my business interests.

No question, Clear Channel is one of the great success stories of the last twenty-five years. Lowry has been diligent from the day we started about informing his directors what the plans are, what changes he is making, and what the future may bring. He is not an "I Did It My Way" kind of guy.

GARY WOODS

I have always reserved the right to make my own mistakes, and many of my associates have obliged me. But not Lowry Mays.

When I went through my hospital stay and my illness with hepatitis, which was complicated by my heavy use of alcohol, Lowry started scolding me almost the moment he realized I wasn't going to die. I had missed a chance to purchase the Houston Astros, an amusement park, and a string of hotels because I was incapacitated.

This was, he pointed out, not a good thing for one who insisted on being a one-man band, as I had been with all of my core businesses. Mays was concerned that I didn't have a right-hand man who worked with me as an overseer of the various entities in which I was involved. Basically, the management line went directly from me to the foot soldiers. I had no *capo,* no *consigliere.*

Mays spent a serious amount of time telling me I needed someone in such a role because of the scare we had survived. It was not a good business practice for me or my family or anyone else not to have a person under me who would be a conduit to all the ventures.

I listened, and I understood his concerns. But I really did not plan to follow his advice. I felt that I had been successful the way I had always done it, and I really couldn't see bringing in someone at such a high level. I had started my businesses out of my hip pocket and let one thing lead to another. They always did.

Mays called me a few weeks later and said, "You have to be the luckiest s.o.b. in the world. I just had a call from a fellow I know in Houston, and he wants to go to work for you. He would be perfect in that role as the president of the holding company and work right under you."

I said, "Lowry, I appreciate that a lot, but—"

"Now, look," he said, "I'm going to have him send you his résumé and I want you to talk to him."

Within a few days I received in the mail a nice letter and a résumé from Gary Woods, who at the time was the chief financial officer and director of a public company. He was a young man with an impressive record, from his educational background (he had a doctorate) up to his executive position with an oil company.

After reading the résumé, I placed it over on the right-hand corner of my desk. People who know me well recognize that this is not a good sign. That corner historically has been a Bermuda Triangle for documents and proposals that just disappear. I didn't think much more about it, until Lowry called back and asked me what I thought of the credentials of Gary Woods.

I said, "About as impressive as I have ever seen."

"What did you do about it?"

"Well, I haven't really done anything with it."

His voice was hesitant. "Don't tell me you put it over on the right-hand corner of your desk?"

"As a matter of fact, I did."

There was an audible sigh. "Red, believe me," he said, "you need to talk to him. I'm going to have him call you."

Gary called and it was, I am inclined to say, just the hand of God that the contact went any further than that phone call because I really had no intention of hiring anyone. Gary sensed as much during the call and suggested that he drive to San Antonio and spend a little time visiting with me. Which he did. Even after we had what might loosely be described as an interview, I was in no frame of mind to make a move.

We reached a point in the discussion where I suggested to Gary, in a nice way, that he was more than qualified for my world. But I really didn't feel I needed anyone in that role, and with his background he would have no difficulty finding exactly what he wanted.

His response was: "I'm not looking for a job. I thought I made that clear to Lowry. I have a great job. I have offers of other jobs, including company presidents. I want to go to work with you."

I was kind of stunned. I asked the obvious question: "Why me?"

"Well, I'm a native of Lockhart (near San Antonio) and I've followed your career. I've been impressed with your programs as an entrepreneur. I have a great background, a very disciplined background in finance, and I think I can learn a lot from your skills. And I hope I can offer something to you. But I'm interested in working with Red McCombs. I'm not looking for a job."

As he was telling me this, and frankly I was pleased by what I heard, I had made a decision. I asked him how much money he was making, and he told me. I said, "If you want to come to work for me for half that much, we will start whenever you want. Since I don't have anyone in a role like this, I don't have any criteria for what the job should be. And I can't tell you if there will be any bonus or not, and that will be at my sole discretion."

Gary said, "That sounds rather harsh, but I'm going to do it."

I decided on the spot that this guy was sincere and wanted to work for me. I would verify it by putting him to a test that hardly anybody could overcome.

I knew after the first week that he was going to serve as a great advantage for me. We chose not to office together. We are not even in the same building. Gary went to work learning all of our investments just by taking my income tax returns and going through them. That was a process he suggested, because after he signed on, my question was: "Where do you start?"

He said, "Well, I know you don't want to spend your time bringing me up to date. Why don't I just take files and start going through them? As I come to questions I will learn as I go." I, too, would have questions for Gary, using his financial background. I knew instantly this was going to be a great combination. Gary doesn't waste words, doesn't spend time jaw-boning, as I am apt to do all the time. He gets to the meat of the coconut quickly. His skills are monumental. By the end of the first year, I was so impressed by what he had done that I saw to it he was compensated many times over from the salary with which he started.

Gary has been involved as a partner in many of my ventures. He is more than a partner—he has become a part of our family. There is no possible way I could have done half the things I've done since Gary joined me, if he had not been there.

In the scary financial times of the late 1980s and early 1990s, I don't believe my skills alone would have helped us survive the crises without Gary's expertise. He has advised me at times against some of the ventures I chose. I will say that his advice proved correct about ninety percent of the time. However, he is such a great team player that when I take on an investment he opposes, he gives his all trying to make it work. Even when it doesn't, I have never heard "I told you so."

You would have thought that a bright young guy with a nimble financial mind, who wanted to learn from someone he thought was a master of the entrepreneurial arts, would stay awhile and then go off and start his own companies. He never did that. Gary had capital when he came to me. He had resources. The ventures of mine that he has taken an interest in all have been with him paying for his shares up front.

Fortunately for me, careerwise, I think the arrangement has been satisfactory for Gary Woods. Since the end of that first year, I have always indicated to him that he can have a piece of any of the businesses. His selections are the ones he chooses to be involved in. His record, I must say, is much better than mine.

GENE McCOMBS

If the world were divided into saints and sinners, one side would be wildly outnumbered. But there is no question where my younger brother would fit. Gene McCombs died in July of 2000 after a painful, twenty-year struggle with lupus. He was sixty-nine and married for forty-nine of those years to the former Mary Broadway, a delightfully ironic name for one who walked beside her husband, with God.

They raised two children, built four churches, and re-cited the 23rd Psalm together every night of their marriage, in sickness and in health.

The first time I ever heard Gene preach, just out of his teens, I predicted he would become an evangelist. The Memphis newspaper, the *Commercial Appeal,* referred in its obituary to his "purity, humility and integrity," adding that these were "not words that come to mind when you think of an evangelist."

He preached across the South and had a good name, if not a big one, as the founder of the McCombs Evangelistic Ministries. He was sweet-tempered, rarely crit-ical—qualities he inherited from our father.

Gene was younger than me by three years and we had a typical big brother-little brother relationship. My total admiration of him really came about when he was in the seminary, training to be a Baptist preacher. He married be-fore I did, and had a beautiful daughter and son.

I shared with him in a minimal way my resources while he attended school. In his second year in the seminary, a mutual friend brought to my attention that Gene was living in absolute poverty. I was not aware of that and immedi-ately went to Fort Worth and found a half-day's supply of food in his refrigerator. He had lost a part-time job and truly was in dire circumstances, which he had never men-tioned. When I asked him what source of income he had, other than the meager amount I was then sending him, he said he had borrowed a hand mower and was mowing lawns. At that time he was the pastor of a church that paid him nothing, and he had the expense of buying gasoline to get there.

As a car salesman, I wasn't exactly running around with hundred-dollar bills falling out of my pocket. Charline joined me in offering to share what we had. We all received more from Gene than we gave.

I was so struck by his faith, and his insistence that he was fine and that everything would be okay, that I embraced him. I made a promise that, for the rest of his life, whatever my living circumstances were, I would commit to him that he would have the same. It was a privilege for Charline and me to be able to share our good fortune with Gene and Mary.

Even though his continuing illness left him close to disabled for the last fifteen years, he was a daily inspiration of faith and hope. Never once was there a negative thought. I was privileged all of my adult life to experience that kind of love from my parents and subsequently from Gene.

I recognized that where God had called him to minister to the people, Gene had been faithful to that commitment in such a way that it was uplifting for me. From time to time I found it easy to look at whatever situation I was in and never feel I had the bad end of anything. With his passing, that impact did not change because every day I refer back to some of his letters that lifted my spirit and continue to play a huge role in my life.

My financial aid had an unexpected consequence. There were times in his ministry when some of his parishioners would question how a poorly paid Baptist minister could live in a fine home, drive a new car, and travel to Europe. The church was paying him only $600 a month. This is a sad commentary, but fortunately not a common one. He was not only a brother but my rock, and I was his supporter. Having loving parents and siblings is a gift of angels.

OILMEN

At the turn of the twentieth century, and again in the 1920s, the world discovered that the drought-stricken fields and pine-studded hills of Texas were floating on an ocean of oil. On a little knob of land called Spindletop, rising out of the swampy prairie a few miles south of Beaumont, in January of 1901, a new age of human progress was born when the first great oil gusher blew in.

Two decades later, a man named Dad Joiner brought in the first wells in what became known as the East Texas Field, and started the greatest treasure hunt America had ever seen. In three days, the dirt-poor town of Kilgore went from a population of 700 to over 10,000 "boomers, desperadoes and hookers." That is how authors Jim Clark and Michel Halbouty described the scene in *The Last Boom.*

There was no law until a Texas Ranger called Lone Wolf Gonzalez rode in to confront, by himself, a growing army of outlaws. This created the agency's battle cry of "one riot, one Ranger."

And the oil derrick became forever the symbol of the state of Texas.

I had always been fascinated by the oil business, as fascinated as anything else in the business world that I ever knew. The fascination began when I was a boy, listening to stories of wildcatters who searched for what they called "black gold."

I had worked as a roughneck on drilling rigs from the time I was in high school through college. But that wasn't where my fascination came from. It came from people who took risks, hit gushers, made and lost fortunes. That was always my fascination. An oil well was the very first thing I invested in when I got out of the University of Texas. While I was in my second month selling cars, I had a fraternity brother who was working as a geologist for a small company in the town of Alice. He asked me if I wanted to participate in a venture they had going. They were drilling a well up near Beeville.

At the time, I was absolutely without any cash. I could put my hands on $400, and I borrowed another $400 from the guys I worked with against my next month's pay. So, at a time when I had no capital to invest whatsoever, I put $800 into a small interest in this well, which, as it turned out, was a natural gas well. We did hit the hydrocarbons, which today would be very successful. But in 1950 the price of natural gas was scraping the bottom, and we didn't have a pipeline in the area. We had to abandon the well, which was the same as a dry hole.

So my first shot at investing in the oil business was a loser. I never lost sight of that experience, and I took small interests in the South Texas wells from the independent producers as I advanced in my career selling cars. When I came to San Antonio in 1958, I met Bill Forney, Sr., in a downtown San Antonio bar that was known as a hangout for oil people. The bar was in the Milam Building, which had mostly oil people as tenants.

I began to invest a few dollars with Bill, who was drilling as an independent operator. These were hit-and-miss deals, which didn't make much money or lose much. Then Bill asked me to finance a lease that he had on a piece of property in South Texas, and *he* determined, not me, that we would become partners.

That connection, which began in 1960, is still carried on today as McCombs Energy. Bill died some fifteen years ago, but fortunately he had two sons who were Oklahoma graduates, as he had been, and the business continued under their leadership. Billy Forney, Jr., operates the company today in Houston. We have been reasonably successful with it, having started all those years ago with no knowledge of the oil business, just my enduring fascination with it.

Over the years, we've had our share of opportunities. Some have turned out good, some have been dry holes. I intend to continue in the business and still see it as a jar that is half full. In a recent period of twelve months, McCombs Energy participated in the drilling of some sixty wells, which is a substantial and ongoing investment.

Going to the well site was really a very exciting part of all this when I first started, but I haven't gone to one in years. I just want to get the report. Did we get the hydrocarbons? How much pressure do we have? It is something that plays a part in my life every day. I'm in contact with Billy Forney on a daily basis. The search for oil and gas, and the history of it, will always fascinate me.

HOLLYWOOD OR BUST

There was a time when being a schoolboy meant going to the movies, the Saturday matinees, the "B" western shoot-'em-ups. Going to the movies was an event as regular as going to church, if not more so. At a certain point in life, if you have made some money, with equal predictability the movies will come to you.

So it came to pass that Angelo Drossos, who had been my ally in the car wars and with the Spurs, grew friendly with Sam Shulman and Irv Levin. Sam once owned the Seattle Super Sonics. Irv earned a lasting fame by trading teams—he swapped his stock in the Boston Celtics for ownership of the San Diego Clippers, the most tortured franchise in the NBA, then and now (in Los Angeles).

Shulman was in the league when there were only seventeen teams, and at the owners' meetings the votes were usually 16-to-1 against whatever he proposed. He was the only owner I ever heard of who wanted to do away with the reserve clause, which kept players tied to one team for life.

It was Sam who stole Spencer Haywood from the ABA, escalating a conflict that almost wrecked the sport. His fellow owners stopped talking to him, and took him to court. When the leagues merged, the suit was dropped.

But Sam was widely regarded as a bomb thrower. "If a guy in any sport doesn't want to play for Seattle, or Los Angeles, or Buffalo, or any other team, why should he be made to do so because the owners have decided that the reserve clause is good for the game?

"In other businesses of mine," he added, "I sign people to contracts of maybe five years. At the end of that time, they are free to stay or move elsewhere. And life goes on. It would be no different in sports."

This is the way it is today, although I doubt even a visionary like Sam Shulman could imagine how crazily the contracts would escalate. In the year 2001, Tom Hicks, the owner of the Texas Rangers, gave a ten-year deal worth $250 million to one player, a shortstop named Alex Rodriguez.

It probably will not shock anyone to learn that Sam and Irv had made the movie industry their primary careers. They were well known in Hollywood and had taken several creative paths to financing motion pictures.

They developed a program and recommended it to Angelo and me, where the four of us would form a company that would require a substantial cash investment, but also would rely on borrowed and leveraged capital.

This company, specifically, would buy an interest, a percentage, in films already completed. Their thrust was that this would move you away from the risk of the cost overruns of the film because the prints would already be finished, and you would buy a negotiated interest in a finished product. From that safe concept, we would build a substantial company.

My relationship with Sam, Irv, and Angelo existed for twelve years, throughout the decade of the 1980s. During that time, our group bought interests involving multimillions of dollars in maybe as many as seventy-five movies. The fortunes of the company ran hot and cold, and I enjoyed the ride, but I sensed it was time to get off the train.

We had been to bat many times, and the right moment presented itself. We hit a pretty big payoff with *Romancing the Stone,* starring Michael Douglas and Kathleen Turner. Our end came to some $25 million, which erased all of the debt in the venture and left about a million to each of us. I told my partners I was out. They could have my interest for a buck.

The other three insisted that this was not a good business move, mainly because they had their sights on a film they considered a blockbuster. Angelo in particular was upset and angry with me for pulling out, and when we flew home on my private plane he complained all the way from Los Angeles to San Antonio.

"Angelo," I said, "stop yelling." And he yelled at me some more.

I was not as enthused as they were about the prospects for the next big flick. I had no more knowledge, and probably less, than they had, but it was just another business decision that I viewed differently.

My judgment was not based on whether the movie would be a success or not. I was put off by the idea we were veering away from the original plan. The cost was considerably higher than our past investments. My partners were convinced that whether the movie itself appealed to the public or not, the stars would carry it.

The stars were, at the time, very hot properties: Sylvester Stallone and Dolly Parton. The name of the movie was *Rhinestone Cowboy,* one of the biggest losers of all time. So the venture ended with my getting out at the right time.

CHARLINE

There is no trophy heavy enough, no pile of money high enough, no success grand enough to compete with the greatest source of pride in my life: my wife of fifty-plus years and my three daughters and their families. As I have said several times, my goals were never to have the most money or the most businesses or to reach a certain status.

I fully realize the truth of that oft-quoted saying, that the joy is in the journey, not the destination.

It may have been fitting, even poetic, that on the day I gave Charline her engagement ring, we celebrated by going that night to the circus and taking along the son of my boss. The first time Charline met my mother, I had invited her over to help me wash my car.

"'Oh, I'd love to,'" she remembers saying. "He picked me up and we drove to his house and that was when I met his mother, Gladys, who was one of the greatest ladies that ever lived. She ruled the household. Everyone did what Gladys said and she doted on her oldest son. We just clicked right off, but I spent the entire afternoon with hoses and a chamois and sponges, washing his car, and I thought, 'I wonder where we're going tonight ...'

"After we got the car all shiny and clean, he said, 'Well, come on, I'll take you home.' Of course, I'm wet and dirty and I jump into that shiny clean car and he drives me home and walks me to the door. And he said, 'I'll see you tomorrow.' And I thought, 'Hmm ... who is getting to go out in that shiny clean car that I just washed?'

"Don't think his mother didn't take note of that, too. He never thought anything about it. That was Red. He had this breezy, lighthearted way about him. No one ever started out earlier to be independent and resourceful.

"A lot of people look back on their lives and think that the best times were when they were struggling. We just enjoyed what we were doing, the different phases. I look back and only see how things just flowed, and we raised our girls together. If we struggled, I missed it somehow.

"There were a lot of gambles, risks taken, but I had 100 percent confidence in what he was doing. The night we were married, in Corpus Christi, we drove to San Antonio. On the way, on a cold, blustery November night, he started telling me some of his goals and aims and philosophies, all brand new to me. He made one statement that we didn't discuss for many years. I brought it up once, years later, and he was surprised I had remembered.

"He had said to me, 'I want you to be prepared because we are going for a ride! I don't know what life holds for us, but it's going to be great. Some day I may come home and tell you we're going to South America, and I expect you to be supportive.' I said, 'I've always wanted to go to South America.' That was how we started our marriage. I keep reminding him that we've never gotten to South America."

CHAPTER 11

PURPLE PRIDE, PURPLE PASSION

This was an honor, an award so unexpected that I found myself almost speechless. On Thanksgiving Day of 1998, I became the first National Football League owner ever to receive a turkey leg from John Madden, the former coach who reinvented himself as a TV analyst.

The Vikings had defeated the Dallas Cowboys that day, on national television, in Texas Stadium, in my home state. Madden was well known for recognizing those players he regarded as down and dirty, unselfish, willing to play hurt, tough to the bone. Compliments do not get much finer than this, especially for an owner.

So if you will step back about 100 yards, I will explain how it all came together for the greater glory of the Minnesota Vikings.

To begin with, I had no powerful hankering to start

spending my winters in Minnesota, where the well-traveled Lou Holtz once referred to all the natives as having "blond hair and blue ears."

How I acquired the Vikings really was not a case of perseverance or dogged determination on my part. I had been in the hunt for an NFL team in different ways for thirty years, including as the applicant for an expansion franchise for San Antonio in 1992 and 1993. That one ultimately went to Jacksonville, and I pretty much abandoned my hopes of joining the NFL. I believed that time had overtaken me. I no longer dwelled on the idea, because I didn't want to suffer that kind of torture after thirty years of being unsuccessful.

My day-to-day activities were full, my life was contented, and I am not one to keep looking back.

Then, at least two years before the purchase, from an almost accidental source, I became aware that the Vikings might be in play—if not then, soon.

The Fox affiliate in Minneapolis, owned by our company, Clear Channel, suffered a serious loss of revenue as a result of having to black out half a dozen of the Vikings' home games. Rip Riordan, who ran the television division, was based in the Twin Cities. During a phone call, I asked him why a team playing as well as the Vikings had so many games that were not sold out. Rip said, "I just believe they are not taking advantage of all the opportunities that are here."

Long before the Vikings officially came onto the market, I began to investigate the possibility of acquiring them. I thought I had retired from chasing sports franchises. But I was like an old bloodhound who had picked up the scent.

This was a team with an intriguing history. To the surprise of many, the NFL had suddenly decided to expand into Minnesota in 1960, persuading a group headed by Max Winter to renege on a commitment to the upstart American Football League. So the Vikings were born in a cradle of mischief and double dealing.

The AFL persevered, though, and in time the Vikings thrived, up to a point. They reached the Super Bowl four times and lost them all. They became part of the lore of the game: the Purple People Eaters, Fran Tarkenton, Jim Marshall, and coaches as opposite in temper as the explosive Norm Van Brocklin and the placid Bud Grant.

Tarkenton was pro football's original scrambler, a daring escape artist, a little guy sticking his tongue out at the big guys and living on the edge. What he lacked in artistry he made up for with energy and quick feet. He was like a tick: You had to set him on fire to get rid of him.

Jim Marshall was a defensive end, part of the famous front four that included Carl Eller, Alan Page, and Gary Larsen. Jim lasted twenty-three years and landed himself in the Blooper Hall of Fame, in 1964, against San Francisco. In that game he scooped up a fumble, fled sixty-six yards into the end zone, and then joyfully flung the ball toward the stands. It was the lineman's dream come true! Alas, he had landed in the wrong end zone for a safety. It was Columbus discovering China.

Marshall sensed something was wrong when the 49ers swarmed around to congratulate him. Tarkenton was the first to spell it out. "Jim," he shouted, "you ran the wrong way!"

The long, lost run of Jim Marshall captured the essence of the Minnesota franchise for many years.

Now it was 1997, and I had met privately in Minneapolis with the ownership group and their attorney. This did not give me an advantage when they later announced the team was for sale, but we knew each other. When they decided to use the process they did (in effect, creating an auction), I considered it fair to all parties.

Although the media continued to raise the question, moving the team to San Antonio was never on my agenda if I had the winning bid. This was Minnesota's team. I could not see it going anywhere else.

That issue didn't enter into what turned out to be the

first round of bidding. The author Tom Clancy, whose spy novels had become automatic movie hits, appeared to be the winner with a bid of $200 million. I was disappointed, but I had been given a clean shot and had no complaints. I wished him well. The sellers were very considerate and thanked me for being involved, but at that instant I was quite sure the Vikings had been sold to the author of *The Hunt for Red October* and *Clear and Present Danger,* among others.

The first hint I had that the deal might crater was from the media. I read that Clancy had asked the league for an extension in providing certain financial documents. He was involved in a very costly divorce, as many are, and this had further clouded the picture. Still, I was not eager to succeed due to the misfortune of someone else, so it was with mixed feelings that I began to see these reports.

It had been obvious that he was a great fan of the team, and would have brought enthusiasm and celebrity to the ownership. But it was also obvious that there would be no deal. The attorneys notified us that they would be mailing out new applications to anyone who had already shown an interest. In short, the team was on the block again.

My proposal was going to be higher this time, and not because Tom Clancy had raised the bar. The size of the television contract wasn't known when the first proposals were sent in. NBC had dropped out, but CBS, Fox, ESPN, and ABC had assured the league of a total package worth $3 billion for the first of eight years, another record for TV rights.

So we had to factor into the bidding an additional income stream for those eight years. I also realized that in this second go-round, the competition would include Glen Taylor, the owner of the NBA's Timberwolves. I knew there would be strong sentiment for local ownership, as there always should be. I also figured that I was going to have to be substantially higher than the local proposal, and I understood and agreed with that.

In a perfect world, the people who own teams would

live in their respective cities. My experience in not being a local owner had been with the Denver Nuggets and, as with the Vikings, the team had been for sale for a good while. There was ample opportunity for any of the locals to step up, but the team had gone begging.

The deal was attractive to me, if not to so many others. You can't analyze a pro sports team as you would any other business. It is unique, with great risks, over many of which an owner has little or no control. I can see why owning a team would not be your everyday choice of investment. It doesn't offer quite the same security as, say, Treasury bills, but you get a whole lot more carbonation.

Since the time I co-owned the Corpus Christi baseball team, in 1953, I have said that I never invested in a sports team expecting a big return. But I always expected I could stay in the black operating a team, and up to this point I have been successful in doing so.

I don't think anyone, including my wife Charline, really shared my feeling that I would wind up with the Vikings. I just had a definite conviction that it was meant to happen long before it did. Can't tell you why. Don't know why.

On the day the bids were due, the deadline was 5:00 P.M. We had done our diligence on the team, but the sellers didn't know if I was going to submit an offer or not. Gary Woods, my alter ego, had taken a previously planned vacation to Europe. The bankers I worked with at Chase, who had provided a lot of the information I needed from the league, were unsure. I had played it as close to the vest as I could.

Several days earlier I had gone over the terms of the contract and bounced back to the Viking lawyers some issues I had, so there would be no surprises if I did submit a number. I had also gotten them to agree to accept my proposal by fax, meaning I could take it to the wire, if need be.

I knew absolutely that I was going to make a proposal, and what that was going to be. All of the foregoing was simply strategy. I hadn't divulged my intentions to anyone else.

I had gone over some of the issues and terms with our legal department, and at 1:00 P.M. Gary's flight from London had landed in Chicago and he called me from the airport.

I said, "Gary, I am going to send in a proposal around 4:00 this afternoon and I expect it to be successful."

Gary asked the obvious question: How much was I prepared to offer? I told him. "If you really want to close this deal," he responded, "and get this franchise, I think that number is too low."

I said, "Well, I think it's going to be ten to fifteen million dollars higher than the next bidder, and that's what I want it to be."

"You may be right," he said, "but I don't think so."

I ended the conversation by saying, "I have never been so confident about anything in my life. This is going to happen and this is going to be the right number." Then I called the Chase bankers in New York and gave them the news. Their response was the same as Gary's.

"Red, if you want this," one of them said, "you're going to have to raise that price."

My comfort level was off the meter. I have bid on a lot of businesses. Sometimes you have a feel for it; sometimes you don't. In my mind, I knew this was going to work, even though I was the only one who seemed to think that way.

With the deadline set for 5:00 P.M. Wednesday, I assumed that the sellers would gather in their attorneys' offices the next day and exercise extreme care in looking at the offers because of their earlier problems. I doubted that any decision would be made before Thursday, and guessed they would hold the announcement until Monday. So I had booked my calendar solidly for the rest of the week.

Gary returned home from his vacation and called around 11:00 A.M. on Thursday. He had just finished talking to John Moudy, the lead attorney for the sellers, all of whom were sitting in John's office. He had a couple of questions he wanted to ask me.

"Are they questions of substance?" I asked. Gary said they were not. In fact, they were easily answered, lending further weight, he believed, that there would be no decision out of Minnesota that day. I had a totally different take. "You know what I think those two questions mean?" I said. "It means I own the Vikings."

Around noon I was driving back to my office, and my mind was not too focused on my next appointment. The car phone rang and Gary yelped, "Congratulations! John just called and they want to call you between 3:00 and 3:30 to confirm the deal and wish you well."

There I was, in my car on Loop 410, when I realized this quite remarkable event had happened. I immediately called Charline at the ranch in Colorado, and my first words were, "You're going to have to buy a lot of purple for your wardrobe because you're the new owner of the Minnesota Vikings."

She knew this was important to me, reason enough to be excited, although she wasn't quite sure what it all meant. Then reality jolted my reverie. I thought, hey, if those owners are calling me, and there are ten of them, and several people working on the documents in the law firm, this was going to be a news item whether I wanted one or not.

I called Gary and said, "I'm going to invite the news media to a 4:30 P.M. press conference and we're going to announce this before the word leaks out of Minnesota."

I needed help. My next call was to Jim Dublin, who had done so much PR work for us in the past. His office was closed, and every account executive was on vacation except Virginia. I told her I was going to hold a press conference at 4:30. "It's not a good time, the TV news goes on at 5:00, but it's the best I can do." Then I started calling my three daughters. I asked Marsha if she could locate any Vikings' memorabilia, and her husband, John Shields, managed to find a cap, which I perched on a little football helmet that I keep on my desk.

On schedule, I talked to the soon-to-be former owners. I had gotten to know most of them over the years, and had originally indicated to that group, and the media, that I would buy 100 percent of the stock. Or, if anyone wanted to stay in, I would keep a minimum of 60 percent. As I began to get other calls, I started to revisit the NFL requirements and the scrutiny that would be involved. I decided on the spot that I would not be taking on any partners, and I notified all the owners of same. They would have to go through the process again and I did not want any delays. It was July, and the teams were ready to play football. They were all very gracious about it.

Once we started going through the lengthy process of approval, the first indication I had that we had crossed the goal line was when I received a phone call from Tom Benson, who owned the Saints and, ironically, was a close friend who had been a tough competitor in the car business when I started out in San Antonio in 1958.

Tom had been on a conference call with the other members of the executive committee, and although they had not yet met he felt secure in relaying their consensus. "Congratulations," he said, "you've been approved as the new owner of the Vikings."

According to Gary Woods, the NFL approval process was the most intensive of any we had ever experienced. We had the Viking owners saying, very generously, that I could step in and start making decisions, but they had not yet been paid.

In the NFL it isn't easy to get an agreement on whether New York is crowded. It appears that Al Davis will abstain on most issues because of his ongoing legal actions, and two or three other owners can be contrarious. Both Benson and Jerry Jones assured me that the committee's approval was tantamount to getting the league's approval, but you won't get every vote.

When I was called into the room and greeted by the

owners, the commissioner, Paul Tagliabue, had a little lilt in his voice when he said, "You are unanimously welcomed into the league."

This was a unique opportunity. I have never taken it lightly and I don't believe other owners do, either. At the outset, I said to the people of Minnesota: "I'm a fan first and an owner second." I really believe that I represent the thousands of fans who would love to be owners. That's the way fans think about their football teams.

I expected that the fans and the media would have some apprehension about the new custodian, an out-of-state guy who for five years had been actively pursuing a team for San Antonio. I embraced that head-on, knowing the issue would come up time and again.

My first order of business was to fly to Minnesota and let them check me out. I stayed seven days, and asked the Vikings' staff to schedule me with media or fan groups from 6:00 A.M. to 10:00 P.M. that entire week. I had lots of opportunity to tell the story of what my role would be. There was never any question about that. I have a passion for the Vikings. I operate as an owner, not an investor.

Dennis Green was on vacation in California when my offer was accepted, and he graciously volunteered to fly from California and join me for the announcement in Minnesota. I declined that. But from the time of that first phone visit, every conversation I had with Dennis, the more impressed I became.

It had been suggested to me by more than one person that I was fortunate Dennis Green had only one more year left on his contract as coach. They assured me I would not like Dennis. One enduring thing about sports: everybody has an opinion.

I had no preconceived notions, but I knew it would be brought up in my first press conference. It was about the third question: "Red, what are your comments about Green's book?" Dennis had authored a book that had been published several months prior to my purchase of the team, and it had attracted a lot of notice from the media in Minnesota.

My comment was that I had not read Dennis' book nor did I intend to read it.

Next question: "Why not?"

"You guys have written enough about the book," I said, "that I don't want to read it because I want to like Dennis Green." As I got to know him, even on the phone, I recognized his organizational skills. I was impressed that the Vikings had a number of players, about half the team, who were not big names when they came to the Vikings, who had developed into great players under Dennis and his staff.

We probably had about ten conversations by phone. In one of those, I asked him if he had any problem with my being in the locker room. I had been around sports and knew coaches had different feelings. I like to be in the thick of things. He kind of laughed and said, "I'm happy to have an owner who wants to be involved."

The fact is, I bought a much better football operation than I had ever dreamed would be there. On the other hand, the business side, which I expected to be better, was a little disappointing. I've learned that when you buy a business, you're going to have surprises and they are not usually going to be pleasant.

If people looked at the background of Dennis, they would have seen that in his nine years with the Vikings six or seven guys had left his staff to become a head coach or coordinator—a fairly strong endorsement for a coach who hadn't won the Super Bowl.

I had looked forward to addressing the team and all the football people when they were in training camp. My first day in camp, at Mankato, they had just finished an afternoon practice and were already in the locker room. They had never seen me. I had planned on going into the locker room and meeting each of them individually.

After I met the first several who were nearest the doors, I realized there were a hundred and fifty people in there—players, coaches, staff. I could see this was going to be awkward. I'm sure my voice was carrying to every corner of the room, and I saw players coming out of the aisles and into the walkway. Fortunately, I spotted Cris Carter, who had taken off his jersey and shoulder pads and was undoing his pants. At which time I solved my personal dilemma by walking all the way through the middle of the locker room, approaching and saying: "Cris, I'm Red McCombs. Would you mind just turning around slowly so I can look at my money?" Laughter erupted on all sides, and that sort of broke the ice.

We had arranged for me to address the staff and the team in the auditorium, early in the evening, before they went into their breakouts. So we had a nice setting. I asked Dennis, when he presented me to the team, not to go through any introduction. I just wanted him to say, simply, "This is Red, he's the new owner and he wants to say a few words." And that was what he did.

I stood on the stage with about a hundred players and a staff of fifty sitting in the audience, giving me their full attention. I had goose bumps. My remarks to them were very straightforward:

"I am very proud to be one of you, because if you are into football, you and those you play against are the best in the world at what you do. Very seldom does anyone in life have an opportunity to compete at that level. So cherish the moment. Don't take it lightly. You guys have been all stars since you were twelve years old, but this doesn't last forever.

"Recognize it, realize it, enjoy it. Because, yes, you and the guys you play against are the best in the world at what you do." I think we had a special feeling between us from the very first moment.

I was blown away. You've heard it said countless times,

but this is what it's all about. You can talk about All-Americans. You can talk about Super Bowls. But their world is special, because so few ever get there. And I was about to make it my world.

Once I got settled in at training, I really began to look at this team and the league in a slightly different way. I came to the conclusion that there wasn't a game on the schedule the Vikings couldn't win. And the media had a field day with my saying so. Now, I didn't say we were going to go through the season undefeated. What I saw was a team coming out of training camp with a chance to win every week, including the preseason.

To me, all games count. I have a problem with the term "exhibition game." My first question was, "What is the plan for selling out the preseason opener?" The staff response was that the Vikings had never sold out an exhibition game. I said, "Kids in the street play exhibition games. The Vikings play preseason games, and I don't ever want to hear that other word again."

I honestly believed that the fans were not fully aware of the human drama that was unfolding each week. You had a hundred and twenty players trying to win fifty jobs. I went so far as to have our staff prepare a small program with the players in alphabetical order at each position. At the final cutdown we might have three left, so the fans could easily see where the battle was. One or two of these guys wouldn't be there, whatever the number. It's not like in other professions. You don't fall down a notch. You fall off the face of the earth.

My prophecy, or maybe I should call it my fantasy, started to be fulfilled as the season progressed. The press asked me what was first on my agenda. I said to do everything I could to see that the Vikings had the home field advantage. This issue of why teams do so much better at home than on the road is really so simple: a player goes into a sold-out stadium, shades of purple everywhere, ear-popping loud and everyone yelling for him to win. Do you suppose his adrenaline would be pumping a little more than if he went into the opposite situation, where everyone was yelling for him to lose, and get killed?

If you don't have the home field advantage, and have to play against it everywhere you go, then you have a double whammy.

I was on my treadmill at home on Wednesday, before the opening game against Tampa Bay on Sunday. We had won all four of our preseason games, and I was convinced this was a special team, headed for a special year. I was doing a mind job on myself, trying to imagine what could go wrong.

Injuries. You knew you were going to have them, over the course of sixteen games. In key positions you had to have backups who could come in on the next down, not the next game. In my mind, I was going over the roster. Dennis had those holes filled. There wasn't anything we could do about injuries, but we had what we needed in the key backup spots. Key Number 1: Brad Johnson and Randall Cunningham at quarterback.

So, my juices were really flowing and I was thinking, well, what then can go wrong? Then it hit me. If we won our first four and into the Green Bay game undefeated, then the media might make an issue out of Dennis' contract. That being the case, what would we do about it? We had everything going our way, our regular season opener was Sunday, and we didn't want anything to distract the team. I'd already told the media I wasn't going to redo any contracts.

In my case, I got off the treadmill and waited two hours and called the coach's office. "Dennis, this is Red," I blurted out. "I want to extend your contract."

He said, "What are you talking about?"

"I know I said I didn't want to do this, but when I bought the team you didn't know me and I didn't know you. I want to extend your contract. The question is, do you want it extended?"

He said, "Well, of course. That's what I've wanted from the time you bought the team."

"Well, Dennis, I'm going to get on your side of the table, just to be fair. You're going to go to the Super Bowl this year. You're going to be a hot commodity. I want you to think about it."

"Red, if you want to extend my contract, that's what I want."

I said, "Okay, now, I've thought about it a little more than you have because I've been thinking about it for two hours. Let's figure out how we're going to do this, without disrupting the team."

Now, keep in mind, money or terms have not been mentioned. Dennis said, "We'll have our last practice Saturday morning and I will turn the team loose about noon. I will tell the team at that time. I think this is going to be motivational for them, and they will be well pleased."

I said, "Okay, this is Wednesday. We're going to tell the team Saturday, which means we have to tell the media Saturday. Now, I'm going to tell Gary Woods, and you're going to tell your agent, and that means at least four of us will know about it. We can't have this leak until you do your number at noon. I will notify our staff Friday night that I will have an announcement to make Saturday at 1:00 P.M."

It worked out beautifully. The team was excited, the news didn't leak, and we caught a few reporters by surprise. There was every kind of guess in the world, as could be expected.

We extended Coach Green's contract for three years, with a nice raise, and the whole thing was done in half a day. This was not something I had planned on doing, but it was still the best thing to do for the Vikings. The usual perception is that a new owner comes in, says he will review the staff at the end of the year, and that tells you the coach is just about gone.

We began to see a team, week after week, not only winning but having fun. We had sold out not only every game, but every product that we had licensed. I became aware that the Viking brand, as I called it, had a huge following beyond the borders of Minnesota.

I had no reason to know this, of course, until I became a Viking. But wherever I traveled, I became aware that the Vikings were big, and in the midst of a storybook season getting bigger. We had a coach who said he was going to quit, but then several owners said he couldn't quit because they wanted to fire him. We had a quarterback who had been out of football and then came back to have an MVP kind of season in Randall Cunningham. And then we had a rookie with a troubled past, one that other teams had made a different judgment on, and you were able to draft him with the twenty-first pick. Randy Moss was a rookie only in the sense that this was his first year in the league. He was not a rookie as a person or as a football player. We also had a place kicker, Gary Anderson, who set a record with every extra point and field goal; a punter, Mitch Berger, who went virtually unnoticed, who put more balls inside the 20 than had been done in years.

So there were great things happening around this team. And there was one other distinction worth noting: We had fifty guys on the squad and all the coaches and not a jerk in the bunch, which is very rare.

Here was a team that had been reading in the papers about a pending sale, and other conflicts, and it was nothing short of miraculous to have all these athletes come together. That was not a Red McCombs thing. That was a team thing. All I know is what I saw and what I felt.

To me, there were three key games before the killer loss to Atlanta.

The first one was in the fifth week of the season, when we went into Green Bay for a Monday night game on ABC. The Packers had won twenty-five in a row at home, and I was convinced we were going to win and win big.

This was our first trip into Green Bay for Charline and me, and she thought I had totally lost my mind. I spent two hours before the game walking through the parking lot, talking to the tailgaters, just trying to find out what really made up this fascinating program—the secret of this Green Bay mystique. I found tailgaters in the parking lot who did not even have tickets to the game. Some of them had been out there all day, cooking, having fun, loving their team. I was more than impressed. I was touched by this kind of loyalty and feeling.

Even before the game started, I was getting good vibrations. During the warmups, I happened to be talking to Randy Moss, who said, "Chief, you're really going to like this game tonight."

I said, "Well, yeah, I like every game."

"But you're going to especially like this one. It's going to be your kind of game."

"What do you mean?" I asked.

Randy grinned and said, "We're going downtown early and we're going downtown often."

Did they ever. I had been kidding Dennis and the offensive coordinator, Brian Billick, except that I wasn't always kidding, telling them, "Let's simplify this game. On offense, go downtown on every play and on defense, let's blitz." All of which they laughed off, and probably with good reason. At any rate, Randy knew what the game plan was and he knew I would love it, which I did.

The exhilaration of that game, from two hours before it started until it was over, I won't even try to describe. Now we were on a roll and getting into the middle of the season, winning at Green Bay, winning everywhere. We had beaten Tampa Bay at the Metrodome in our opener.

Then with the team unbeaten in seven games, it was time to play at Tampa Bay. And I couldn't go. I was too ill with a virus to get out of bed, and darned if we didn't lose the game, our only defeat during the regular season. There

I was, stuck at home, rumpled and feverish, watching us go down and feeling as if it was almost the end of the world. I never have really tried to claim that I keep sports in perspective, and I won't start now. I don't believe there is a perspective.

But we rebounded and started winning again, and then it was time to go to North Texas on Thanksgiving Day. It was a chance to see a fellow I like a lot, Jerry Jones, one of the absolute best operators in all of sports. Best of all, we would be facing the Dallas Cowboys on national television on Thanksgiving Day in my home state.

I said before the game, I don't know how big a Super Bowl is because I haven't yet done one. For a guy from Spur, Texas, to go into Texas Stadium on Thanksgiving Day, on national TV, and win the ballgame, it doesn't get much better. If there is anything bigger, I'm ready to try it on.

It was becoming pretty obvious to the whole football world that the Vikings were for real. We finished the season 15-and-1, then won our playoff game against the Cardinals. We went into the Atlanta game as confident as any team ever could be. No one took it for granted. We knew that the Dirty Birds were 14-and-2 for the season and had won their first playoff game. Still, it was a contest every Viking expected to win. I certainly did.

Even as we went into overtime, when luck was with us and we won the coin toss, I turned to Charline and said, "We will score on the first possession," which I fully expected to happen. As it turned out, we didn't score on the first or second possession and, in fact, the Falcons did. I give them all the credit. They came into a very hostile environment, came from behind several times and hung in there. They did the greatest thing you can do in sports: persevere and win.

But it was not anything I could even imagine. I can't weigh or measure that kind of hurt. I will never get over it.

I won't have another chance to be a rookie owner, with a once-beaten team, bound for the Super Bowl.

As the Falcons connected on their field goal to win, I turned and caught the look on the faces of my two youngest grandchildren. And I realized that we had never discussed with them what losing meant. Knowing that I was heading for the locker room, I turned to Charline and pleaded, "Honey, will you please explain to these youngest grandkids what has happened here?"

We had been through this joyous season, this magical sleigh ride, and there was never any thought that we might lose. It was a tough time for everybody concerned. The players had every kind of reaction in the world.

The midterm gubernatorial elections were on November 2, 1998, eight games into the season. It turned out to be a wildly interesting time. The law firm I had retained in Minnesota had advised us that this would be a close election, hard to tell whether the Democrat or the Republican would win. From my standpoint, and wanting to get acquainted with the leadership in Minnesota, I arranged in the early part of the season to entertain Hubert Humphrey, Jr., the Democrat, and the Republican, Norm Coleman, as guests of Charline and me. It never entered my mind to invite the Reform Party candidate, Jesse Ventura, the flamboyant former wrestler.

The night of the election, sitting in our home in San Antonio, Charline and I were watching the election results, concentrating on the Texas races. I noticed a runner at the bottom of the screen that said, "Possible big upset in Minnesota."

I didn't think much about it. Seconds later, the runner said, "Big, big upset in Minnesota . . . Ventura elected governor." At which point, I turned to Charline and said, "Man, have I got my work cut out for me tomorrow." She asked why. I said, "The governor of any state, that's an important person, and this being an upset I haven't even taken the time to meet the guy." So the very first thing the next morning, I called the Vikings' office and said, "Get me on the line with Jesse Ventura." The secretary's response was, "That may be rather difficult. From what we understand, the media is coming in from all over the United States." I told her to do the best she could.

We got lucky. An hour later, the Vikings' office called back and said, "We talked to a member of his staff and he's going to do a radio call-in show that he hosted up to two years ago. He wants you to call him at this number at 12:30." I said, "Great!"

The conversation went something like this: Jesse is talking over the radio and I can hear what he is saying. "By the way," he tells his listeners, "three weeks ago I went to take my family to a Vikings' game and I couldn't even get nosebleed seats. Now, guess who is on the phone calling me? Red McCombs from San Antonio, Texas. Red, do you have any comment on that?"

Talk about eating crow. My reply was, "Yes, I do. Congratulations, Governor. From this day forward, as long as I own the Vikings, you can have any seat in the house. In fact, we'll be playing a game Sunday and I would like to invite you and your family as my guests for the game."

And Jesse said, "You know, I've been into this campaign so much, I really haven't paid that much attention. Are you playing at home or on the road Sunday?" I said, "Jesse, we're playing wherever you want us to play. But, in fact, we're playing in the Metrodome." He said, "Well, by gosh, we'll come and join you."

So the new governor and his two kids came as our guests and saw a great halftime show down on the 50-yard line as 65,000 people screamed and hollered for Jesse. I enjoyed visiting with him during the game, and since that time I've appeared on several programs with him.

I thought he turned out to be a good governor, especially when you consider that Minnesota is a partisan state, with the Republicans in control of one part of the legislature and the Democrats the other. He was a third-party candidate with no established base. This was not the easiest atmosphere to work in, but he started strong.

And, of course, the same could be said for his state's pro football team.

The above thoughts were composed in spring of 2002, and I bring them up to date now, with clearly mixed emotions.

Jesse Ventura announced that he would not run for re-election; he was tired of fighting losing battles. But such an option is unacceptable for the Vikings, who will regroup and move on.

When the good times are rolling in sports, you think they will never end. But, like puppy love, they always do.

As warm and open as my relationship with Dennis Green had begun, it ended obviously in a negative way.

I sensed that something was happening to our friendship after the last game of the 2000 season, when we lost to the New York Giants for the conference championship and a berth in the Super Bowl. We were blown away, 41-0, at the Meadowlands. The loss was a huge and bitter one for all of the Vikings. Among other things, we were heavy favorites, in double digits, to win the game.

Not only did we lose, we really did not compete. Although no specific words crossed between Dennis and me, we never really got back on the same page from that point on.

There is a momentum to losing, just as there is with winning, and you start to expect bad things to happen. When training camp rolled around in July, the team suffered a blow that made all else seem trivial. On the second day of camp, the popular Korey Stringer died of a heat stroke. He was twenty-seven, twice a pro bowler, in his sixth season as an offensive tackle.

I felt guilty even thinking or talking about him in football terms. He was a dear person, devoted to his family, his wife Kelci and his son Kodie, and steadfast to his friends. In my statement to the public, I said, in part, that he was a true professional, a model of "dedication and preparation. He led by example. Words can hardly begin to express our sadness and grief."

His death changed the look and feel of the camp. This is the hard reality of sports. A friend had died, yet his teammates couldn't afford to start thinking that what they do no longer matters. Everyone had to work through that, and we tried to handle the tragedy as best we could, for the Stringer family and the players. There isn't a rulebook that covers such circumstances.

One way to show your respect is to carry on. By the end of the preseason schedule, it looked as if we might be getting back into a football mode. For the first time since I bought the club, we won all four of our preseason games. The 2001 season, I thought, was going to right itself and we would have a legitimate shot, again, to play for the Super Bowl. My early optimism took a pretty good jolt when we lost our opener at home to Carolina, which turned out to be the only game the Panthers won, losing their next fifteen.

The season turned out to be a rollercoaster kind of experience. We lost the second game in Chicago by a score of 17-0. Then we started winning, beating Tampa Bay at home, 20-16, and playing quite well. We lost at New Orleans but came back to win against the Lions in the Metrodome.

I was thinking that we would be able to use the leadership of Dennis to put the program back together. But the team kept slipping and sliding, with the strain and pressure building with each loss. We didn't win a game on the road. In the last month, it was all downhill.

Still, having said that, I was totally surprised by a message I received several days before our last game in Baltimore, on Monday Night Football. I received by fax a memorandum from Coach Green's attorney indicating that there were management issues that very much concerned Dennis.

I was surprised, but not entirely. Still, getting a memo from a lawyer, when you thought you had an open door, was just one level above getting a letter addressed to occupant. Dennis and I never got to discuss those issues because from that point on we had no direct contact.

It became obvious to me on Friday morning, before the Monday night game, that decisions had to be made. Dennis still had two years left on his contract, and the contract speaks for itself. The issue for me was, how were we going to run our football club? We informed his lawyer that a change would be made.

I flew to Minnesota. Dennis handled the practice that Friday morning, then met with the players immediately after practice and announced to them, and subsequently the public, that he was no longer employed by the Minnesota Vikings. I followed that disclosure an hour later with an announcement that I had selected Mike Tice, who had been on the staff for the past six years, to take over the head coaching duties for Monday night's game.

The situation was awkward for all concerned, but I was proud of Mike Tice for accepting a role that he had not sought nor expected. I was proud of the players for responding and playing hard against Baltimore, the defending Super Bowl champion, and keeping it close for three quarters.

Not many weeks later, I named Mike Tice the head coach of the Vikings. I was impressed with the way he put together his staff. I felt excited, again, about the 2002 season.

The only head coaching job Mike had held, prior to his debut on Monday Night Football, before a national television audience, was when he coached his son's seventh-grade team in a YMCA league. This represented a quite spectacular leap for the former six-foot-seven tight end who finished his playing career in Minnesota, after ten seasons with Seattle and one with Washington.

I predict that his unlikely leap will lead to a spectacular coaching career. True, I always feel this way when I have made unconventional choices, at a time when I did not expect to have to make them. This was the case when I hired John Lucas to replace Jerry Tarkanian with the Spurs. I had to make the same kind of quick decision with Dennis Green, and Mike Tice, or allow the speculation about our coaching uncertainty to turn into a media event, and dominate the Monday night telecast.

There is no doubt in my mind that Dennis will continue his coaching career, and I have no doubt that he will be successful. I wish him nothing but the best.

The other continuing story of the 2001 season was: What really happened to Randy Moss? The question rolled through our ranks like a bowling ball wrapped in barbed wire.

Drafting Randy with the twenty-first pick in the first round in 1998, of course, turned out to be a bonanza for the Minnesota Vikings. Randy was exceptional in every way, and was recognized at the end of his rookie season by the records he set as a receiver, which are still records in his fourth year.

But Randy's performance was not on par with past seasons, and a good deal of attention was focused on his new contract, a multimillion-dollar package with an $18 million signing bonus.

The bonus was spread over several years, but the first installment of $5 million was paid before the 2001 season, raising a question that is inevitable in anything as visible as professional sports. Did this big contract play a role in the dropoff in Randy's results?

I recognize that this idea of the Fat Cat Syndrome will

always be open to argument, but I don't think so. The minimum contract in the NFL today is around $250,000. Kids come out of college, where they have been scrambling for gasoline money, and at twenty-one they feel rich overnight, whether the contract is for a few million or a bunch of millions. In my opinion, the magnitude of the money doesn't matter. Even at the minimum, each player is rich overnight on a relative basis.

I don't think his contract was an issue with Randy. There were other issues that troubled him, and troubled me. It was obvious that Randy did not have the opportunities to catch the ball that he had before, and he was frustrated by it. Unfortunately, his frustration led him to make comments at midseason that would cause another distraction the team didn't need.

In an interview with Sid Hartman, one of the most respected sports columnists in the business, he was quoted as saying that he only played "when I want to." Randy never denied saying it, never offered any alibi.

But he was branded with a label that critics were eager to pin on him: a gold brick, a guy who went hard only when it suited him. That isn't Randy Moss. I think he meant that the money didn't dictate how he played; his pride did. I know him as a competitor who wants to win as much as anyone on the team. He goes hard in practice and he works hard in games.

Trying to read a player's mind can cause blurred vision and migraines, but I believe Randy Moss will reestablish himself as the most dangerous receiver in the game, by letting his hands do his talking.

CHAPTER 12

TO SAVE A CHILD

The late Sam Rayburn, longtime U.S. Speaker of the House and legendary Texan, once said: "Readiness makes for opportunity. Opportunity often comes by accident. Readiness never does."

Let me tell you about an opportunity that came into my life at a perfect time. Not a deal. But a chance to do some major selling. I was selling hope and the value of hard work to a tough crowd of kids.

In the mid-1990s, I received a letter from a teacher at Mary Hull Elementary, on the north side of town, high on the list of San Antonio's "at-risk" schools. The students' grades were among the worst in the state, and scores on standardized tests were near the bottom in the nation. About 85 percent of Mary Hull's 572 students came from homes that were below the poverty line.

The teacher who wrote me was formerly a highly paid management professional who decided she would be more fulfilled as an educator. She loved her work and had volunteered to teach in an at-risk school. She asked me if I would come out one day and encourage her fifth-grade class, as they prepared to graduate into middle school. Several weeks after my visit, I noticed a small story in the Sunday newspaper that three classrooms had been torched at Mary Hull. Something of a connection to those kids led me to drive out there early Monday morning.

Since the fire happened on the weekend, no one was hurt. But the school couldn't open. I spoke to the principal, Robert Zarate, and asked what needed to be done. In sports jargon, I asked, "Do you have a game plan?" They needed every kind of help.

One thing led to another, and I offered some of my people and funds to quickly clean the place up and allow the kids to return to class. I was impressed by Zarate's leadership and the fact that he had chosen to work in a school that was on the state accrediting agency's hit list. They either had to meet the standards or shut down. Zarate had adopted a take-charge approach to turning the school around. I began to work with Roberto and the teachers, and the relationship grew over the years. The school adopted me, and I adopted them.

(Zarate told Sunni Scarlett, a writer for a San Antonio business magazine: "When the kids see Mr. McCombs, they scream his name and hug him and almost knock him over. They treat him like a rock star. When (he) makes a commitment, it's personal. His door is always open and he always follows through.")

One of the first challenges the faculty faced was to raise the scores on the Texas Assessment of Academic Skills test, known as TAAS. As an incentive, I offered the students a field trip to the zoo if they succeeded. I knew from the teachers that they were bearing down, concentrating, turning it into a mission. The state test results are not immediately available, and I didn't want the kids to wait for them.

So, confident of the outcome, I sent nine air-conditioned city buses over to the school, and provided them with tickets, lunch, and a memento of the trip.

When the scores came back several weeks later, Mary Hull Elementary was named a Blue Ribbon School by the U.S. Department of Education—one of only 21 in Texas and 263 nationally, out of thousands.

Long ago I learned never to give up on a child. He or she may have a learning disability, may be hyperactive or withdrawn, or the product of an unstable home. But sometimes, if you try, you can look right into a child's heart and see the lights come on.

I made it a point to read to the students on a regular basis. I would give awards to the ones who excelled, and talk to them about why they needed to help each other. The kids who have an easier time learning were encouraged to help the ones who struggle. They would bond and each would grow.

Meanwhile, I was able to reward them by inviting the entire school to my ranch at Johnson City for lunch. Another time we took them all to IMAX to see the whale movie when they were studying the ocean, and to the livestock show for special programs. With the cooperation of the Josephine Theater, we arranged for the cast of "My Fair Lady" to give an exclusive performance at Mary Hull. These were mainly local actors who had day jobs, but the whole cast appeared for an audience of 400 students. They explained how you prepare for a part, and the backstage crew demonstrated setup and props.

There is, or should be, a touch of the dreamer in each of us. The dream begins, most of the time, with a teacher who believes in you, who tugs and pushes and leads you on to the next level, sometimes poking you with a sharp stick called truth. Good teachers earn a kind of immortality. They stay with you for the rest of your life, and later you always intend to go back and visit, except you rarely do. They understand.

My third- and seventh-grade teachers had a strong influence on me. I had college professors who certainly made an impression, but my real interest in education came from my mother and those two teachers. In the third grade, I thought school was for fun and a place to get your hand slapped with a ruler. Mrs. Wadzek saw through all of that and encouraged me to raise my sights, to see how much fun it was to do positive things. She showed me that I didn't have to be involved in mischief to enjoy school. The fact that she was the wife of the high school football coach had a lot to do with it, because that put her close to hero status.

It became important that I please her. She made me realize how much fun it was to fix something, instead of breaking it down; how to travel the world through books.

My mother believed in education, not only as a way to stay out of trouble and to learn life skills, but as a child's best chance to escape the lower rungs of society. She had graduated from high school when that was not a priority for girls in the poor, rural Southwest. She was an avid reader, and to the pleasure of both of us coaxed me into reading to her. To her, education didn't end when school let out. You started over every day. You learned as much as your brain could hold, up to the point of actually feeling pain.

My seventh-grade teacher, a Miss Francis, introduced me to classical literature and inspired me to reach beyond my limited understanding of the world and read outside my experience. Doing so, she said, would stir your thought processes. She could tell if my interest was wandering, and she would ask the questions that made me think: What is the author saying? What point is being made?

I wish everyone had the desire, and the freedom, to volunteer their time at schools. The National Football Foundation sponsors a program called "Play It Smart," in which academic coaches work with high school football players, mentoring them in their studies and making them aware of the importance of being involved in the community. The idea is spreading across the country.

Education is where the young and ambitious go to find opportunities. We need to resolve the issues that have been studied and debated for so long: safer schools, higher pay for teachers, better tools for learning.

In addition to the satisfaction you get from expanding your own knowledge, the educated person is more able to contribute to his or her community. The more involved you are, the more you realize there are people willing to help out as volunteers in their own school districts. They only need to be asked.

I know what I do is not unique. When I was a child, I saw my parents share whatever they had. It wasn't anything unusual then, and I don't think it is today. People have to determine their own comfort level in how they spend their time and financial resources. You should try to reach a level equal to the joy you receive in return.

My father was a farm boy with a third-grade education, but he was very bright. He was an auto mechanic who earned the respect and gratitude of the town because of his skill at diagnosing and fixing problems with motors. He could repair all kinds of equipment, and in a rural setting that person is essential. Like a doctor, he would get phone calls at all hours of the night.

Yet it was in spite of his occupation, not because of it, that I wound up in the car business. As a boy, all I knew about my father's job was that he worked from sunrise to sunset. I didn't see much that was irresistible about that.

I do not consider myself one who is quick to jump on a soap box, but, yes, I brake for at-risk school kids. I have tried to give honest and realistic thought to the problems of public education, and one conclusion I have reached is this: To turn this issue into a family values campaign, as we have seen in recent political cycles, is misleading. Those who go around preaching it are missing the boat because they keep thinking about the family of the 1950s. They are thinking about Ozzie and Harriet.

We need to worry about who is going to act as the surrogate family of the future. Politicians keep talking about the ideal family of four or five decades ago. I don't see anyone going beyond that. I don't see them showing the right kind of courage.

I have investigated the notion of legalizing drugs in our society, after the dismal failure of the war on drugs. My thought is to look at alternatives, because drugs are more available and cheaper today than they were thirty years ago, despite all our efforts. I have discussed this with leaders in business and government I respect a great deal. They would rather talk about education.

If you walk into any classroom in America and write "d-r-u-g-s" on the blackboard, the kids will say, "Don't do it. It will kill you." The kids already know this, yet the problem is still with us in a bigger way than ever. Legalizing drugs may not be the answer. But I would like to see the profit motive and violence it causes to be taken out of the equation.

I consider Henry Cisneros, the former mayor of San Antonio and secretary of Housing and Urban Development, the most effective politician I have ever known. I brought up the subject with Henry, and he thought I was out of my mind. "Oh, Red," he said, "a culture can never give in to this. Do you want your people showing up at work stoned all the time?"

I told him, "There is a liquor store on every corner, and my people don't show up for work drunk."

This debate will continue well into the future. But for now the test is not to abandon our schools, but to adopt them. We need to save this generation of children, and let the lights come on.

EPILOGUE

There is no way to be modest about this. I have received a few surprises in my lifetime, but none to equal the one that fell on me in December of 2001. The National Football Foundation presented me with its highest honor, the Gold Medal.

To put this award in perspective, all anyone needs to know is that the first five recipients were Dwight Eisenhower, Douglas MacArthur, Amos Alonzo Stagg, Herbert Hoover, and John F. Kennedy. Other honorees included Byron (Whizzer) White, John Wayne, General Norman Schwartzkopf, Jackie Robinson, and Presidents Nixon, Reagan, Ford and George Bush, the elder.

It isn't my place to argue with the selection committee. Jon Hansen, the chairman of the foundation, spoke of my "commitment to many worthy causes," and I can accept this tribute because I know I wasn't picked for my achievements as a football player.

You couldn't grow up in Texas, certainly not as a young male in the 1940s, without developing a love of the game. After finishing high school at seventeen, I hitchhiked across the state in the summer of 1945, trying to find a college that would give me a scholarship. I made a tour of six or seven campuses and was rejected by most of the coaches on sight. Then, to my delight, I thought I had made the squad at Baylor, which didn't have a team at the time but planned to renew the sport since World War II was ending. I had made it through two weeks of a training camp, big and willing and naive, raw as a crate of turnips.

After the last day's workout, Bill Henderson, the athletic director and acting football coach, called me in with another ragged candidate. We were the last players to be cut. "You two kids can't help us," he said, as gently as he could, "but I've fixed it for you to go to school if you want."

He said we had a choice of scholarships at Southwestern or Tyler Junior College. I asked him if Southwestern was a four-year school. He said, yes. I asked where it was. He said, "Just down the road at Georgetown." I said, "I'll go there." I will always be grateful for Bill Henderson's help and kindness. That was the start of my education. I was the first member of my family, on either side, to attend college.

I will always be grateful to Southwestern for giving a scholarship to a mediocre athlete. I'm *not* being modest when I say that. I played both ways in the line, then enlisted in the army in 1946. For eighteen months, part of it served in Korea, I sent half my pay home and when I returned had enough for a new car. I enrolled at Del Mar Junior College in Corpus Christi, and played one more season of football. Then I exercised my veteran's option to attend the University of Texas.

My career as a player was over, but not my career as a fan, an observer, and would-be insider. And I was already establishing a pattern, working several jobs to pay expenses and create a cash flow. On a summer break I sold used cars and discovered I was good at it. Everything that followed— investments in cattle ranches, oil and gas, motion pictures, a multi-media company, two NBA teams, and the Minnesota Vikings—all started with one flattering fact: people would buy a used car from me. Or a new one.

Which made it possible to do good deeds. The McCombs Foundation, I read somewhere, gives $8 million annually to some 400 charities and colleges.

Over the years, I supported the University of Texas football program and formed a lasting friendship with Darrell Royal, whose teams never had a losing season in twenty years. I was a kind of bird dog for Darrell during the recruiting season, and he let me do a little light scouting on Friday nights in the San Antonio area, although I was never quite certain what I was looking at.

In time, Charline and I were able to make significant gifts to the business schools of both my universities and build a women's softball stadium at Texas. We had decided at the start of our marriage that we would share our resources, when we had resources to share.

These were among the thoughts and memories that spun through my mind that night in December, as 2,700 guests filled the floor and mezzanine of the grand ballroom at the Waldorf Astoria Hotel in New York. The night was made even more meaningful when the College Football Hall of Fame inducted three coaches I had known and enjoyed: Grant Teaff, who gave Baylor its first Southwest Conference title in fifty years; Bill Yeoman, who invented the Veer offense at the University of Houston; and Barry Switzer, who won three national titles at Oklahoma (and a Super Bowl with Dallas).

Among the fifteen players inducted were Anthony Carter of Michigan and a former Viking; Jon Arnett of USC; Ralph Guglielmi of Notre Dame; and Steve Young of Brigham Young and the 49ers.

To be honored, to be recognized, in such company proved to me again that you can make a difference without making history or headlines. Some people give lots of money. Some give their time. Others organize the ones who give. All ways help.

I have no idea what happened to the other young football player who was cut by Baylor in the summer of '45. But I do know that he missed one incredible night at the Waldorf in December of 2001.

SOURCE ACKNOWLEDGMENTS

For the events, people, and places described in this book, I have relied almost entirely on my memory and personal files. I am comfortable with having done so, especially in the case of those long-ago times for which documents were scarce or non-existent. For their coverage of me, my teams and businesses, and the kind words they included, I wish to acknowledge the following publications, which were extremely helpful as sources for checking facts and dates.

American Academy of Achievement, bio, 1999.

Automotive Executive Magazine, "Double Play" by Dale Buss, 1989.

Associated Press.

Austin American-Statesman.

Business, S.A., Sunnie Scarlett, 1999.

Conquest Quarterly, M.D. Anderson by Mary Jane Schier, 1995.

Corpus Christi Caller-Times, Ellen Bernstein, 1998.

Dallas Morning News, "Man of Many Talents" by David McLemore, 1996.

Dallas Morning News, Brad Townsend, 1998.

Dealer Magazine, Q&A by Michael Roscue, 1998.

Dealer Business Magazine, "Top 100" by C.D. Bohon, 1995.

Forbes Magazine, "Making Money's Fun" by Tedd A. Coben, 1980.

Philanthropy Magazine, Carol Van Natta, 1996.

San Antonio Business Journal, "Top 50," 1996.

San Antonio Current, "Fourth and Long," by W. Scott Bailey, 1996.

San Antonio Express News, "(Giving $5 Million) Just Makes Me Feel Good," by Charlotte Anne Lucas, 1996.

San Antonio Express-News, "Industry Honors McCombs" by Patricia Konstam, 1996.

San Antonio Express-News, "Gift to Empire Project" by Mike Greenberg, 1997.

San Antonio Express-News, profile of Charline McCombs by Paula Allen, 1998.

San Antonio Express-News, "S.A.'s Headliner" by David King, 1998.

San Antonio Light, "Big Red" by Susan Yerkes, 1986.

San Antonio Light, "Simply Red" by Brad Townsend, 1991.

San Antonio Magazine, profile by Tom Walker, 1988.

San Antonio Magazine, "Man of the Year" by Tom A. Porter, 1990.

Scoreboard, Longhorn Foundation, 1997.

Southwestern Quarterly, bio, Red and Charline McCombs, 1997.

INDEX

About the Cover Photographer

OSCAR WILLIAMS specializes in photographing people on location for advertising, corporate, and editorial publication. His photographs capture the unique spirit of each individual. "I enjoy people," he said. "It makes my job easier. If a photograph looks like it took a lot of work to create, I haven't been successful. I simply try to capture the essence of a subject with ease and clarity."

Oscar works with both local and national companies, including USAA, NationsBank, Southwestern Bell, Associated Milk Producers, and Critical Air Medicine. Numerous advertising agencies rely on him as a quality source for photo illustration. Awards have included those presented by the San Antonio Advertising Federation, the New York Art Directors Club, the International Association of Business Communicators, and the Communications Arts Society of San Antonio (CASSA). Oscar has served as a part-time faculty member at Trinity University, his alma mater (BA 1976), and is currently president of CASSA and a founding officer of the Austin/San Antonio Chapter of the American Society of Magazine Photographers.

Oscar Williams, Photographer
202 Lazywood Trail
San Antonio, TX 78216-7068
Phone: (210)342-7600
Fax: (210)342-7630
www.oscarwilliams.com